Accidental
MOTIVATION

Embracing Fate &
Finding Happiness

JOHN HOLSINGER

Library of Congress Cataloging-in-Publication Data
Names: Holsinger, John, author.
Title: Accidental Motivation / John Holsinger.
Identifiers: LCCN 2023921887 (print)

ISBN 13: 979-8-9895322-0-9 (Paperback)
ISBN 13: 979-8-9895322-1-6 (Ebook)

First Edition

To all those who are on a journey to find happiness,
this memoir is dedicated to you.

May my experiences and insights provide a roadmap to help
you understand your purpose and find true joy and fulfillment.
May you find the courage to pursue your dreams and live life
to the fullest, and may this memoir serve as a reminder that
happiness is within reach for all of us.

CONTENTS

INTRODUCTION

We've all heard the saying that life's a journey with its share of expected and unexpected twists, and both play a role in shaping our reality, sometimes in the blink of an eye. Our day-to-day experiences mold us into who we are, but there are also those profound moments that forever change our life's course.

My childhood was spent in the simplicity of a small Ohio town, flying kites and playing outdoors until sunset. At ten, I was thrust toward adulthood by circumstances that transformed me into the man of the household and sparked a lifelong quest for control of everything that I thought had the potential to cause disorder.

Entering adulthood, a job at IBM granted me early access to the unlimited possibilities presented by the Internet, allowing me to literally and figuratively grasp the timeless adage that knowledge is power. This digital gateway connected me to people and ideas across the globe, opening doors I never knew existed. Marriage and parenthood brought joy but also great challenges. As I navigated life and largely experienced success, I was ultimately forced to confront my disillusionment with the American Dream. I found myself pondering questions like: What is the purpose of life? Why am I unhappy? How can I find happiness?

How can one answer these questions, along with the question of whether we have any control?

My pursuit of answers led me to develop a life philosophy that the only reason to live is to be happy and to embrace the selfishness that is required to be so. Though my journey was often fraught with setbacks and trials, my philosophy of Selfish Determinism eventually became my guiding light, but it wasn't until my

"Accidental Motivation" forced me to fully embrace its principles that my transformation truly began from an unhappy, unfulfilled man to one who loves life and feels happy in a way I never thought possible.

Through the pages ahead you'll journey with me, gaining insight into the resilience, pain, and courage that emerged from surviving a traumatic accident and gave me the strength to be curious and discover who I was. It's a story that celebrates the power of growth and reminds us that even amidst life's greatest challenges, we possess the capacity to triumph and find our own unique path to happiness.

A RUNNER'S ACCIDENT

*Accidents happen. You just don't let yourself believe
they will happen to you.*

A to ANNO.

Scott Birk, a prominent figure within Austin's running community, stood as a seasoned and dedicated runner. His remarkable
achievements included completing thirty-seven marathons, twen-
ty-eight half marathons, and fifty-two 5Ks—twenty-two of which
he accomplished in the year 2010 alone. Scott knew how to run,
he ran fast, and he ran nimbly. He had the ability to skillfully
navigate past slower runners, potholes, bicyclists, pedestrians,
and vehicles. Despite his admission that training runs weren't his
favorite endeavor (a sentiment shared by many), his commitment
to achieving results was undeniable. Scott consistently ran over
fifty miles per week, accumulating thousands of miles over his
lifetime. In short, he was one hell of an athlete.

During a training run in the summer of 2011, Scott attempted
to cross a four-lane road but collided with a Dodge Durango.
Tragically, he was pronounced dead at the scene shortly thereafter.
According to the authorities, the driver of the vehicle held the
right of way with a green light when Scott unexpectedly ran in
front of the truck.

Seated at my desk in my home office on that fateful June 13th, I received a phone call from a close friend and neighbor. "Scott was hit by a car, and it sounds serious. He could have lost his life . . . but I'm not sure. Where? At the entrance to River Place. Unimaginable. When did you last see him? What are you going to do?" I found myself staring through the window, grappling with the weight of the news. *Could he really be gone? Surely, he must still be alive . . . friends don't just die, not like that. One moment on a training run, the next it's all over.* He was young, and from my perspective had his whole life ahead of him.

Questions about Scott's situation inundated my thoughts but I had no answers. I also pondered, *what if it were me?*

As runners, we know the distances of the core segments of our routes. In my case, I knew the intersection of the accident was two miles from my home. The notion of heading to the accident scene fleetingly crossed my mind, yet what purpose would it serve? Scott was likely already en route to the hospital and visiting that intersection would only fuel my morbid curiosity. The thought was quickly dismissed. I needed to grapple with my own disbelief.

I picked up the phone and shared the news with my former wife and a couple of friends. "Have you heard about Scott? I can't wrap my head around it. What happened? What exactly happened?" It felt as if I were trapped in the Twilight Zone, having the same conversation repeatedly. "How could this happen? Why did it happen? No, I'm as clueless as you are."

The intersection where the accident occurred was known for previous automobile accidents. My thoughts painted a scenario of one car colliding with another, leading to an impact that could involve an aware and stoplight-respecting Scott on the sidelines. The likelihood of Scott, or anyone for that matter, being present at the precise moment of such an accident was almost inconceivable, but even more inconceivable was the notion of Scott running in front of an oncoming vehicle. And if something so random, so unthinkable happened to him . . .

For much of my life, I have been a recreational runner, training five to ten hours per week. I first met Scott at local social gatherings, yet our encounters were more frequent during training runs or post-race discussions. The route Scott took on the day of his tragic accident was one I had run countless times. In our hilly neighborhood, many endurance athletes (myself included) had to cross that very intersection to extend their run distance. Following the accident, everyone who had a connection with Scott, and fellow runners in a unique way, experienced a profound impact. The sorrow was undeniably painful, and my relationship with Scott intensified the grief. The fact that it happened to a runner, like me, shook the very core of my being. I have rarely run since then without thinking something like that could happen to me, on any given day, during any run.

Scott had no control over the car's presence, the timing of the traffic lights, the driver's actions, or any other aspect of the situation, including his presence at the precise moment of the tragedy. Given the opportunity, he would have undoubtedly made different choices—just as anyone would have. He could have opted to stretch on the sidewalk, chosen an alternate route, or taken a day of rest. The "could've" and "would've" scenarios loom large. I'm certain that Scott would have taken any action necessary to avoid the accident had he known he would be struck by a car and lose his life.

Hindsight often renders many things possible or seemingly foolish. In the moment, our thoughts appear logical to us, driven by our individual reasons for making specific choices. Had anything been different, the accident would never have happened. Scott likely considered various types of information—his running pace, the intersection's speed limit, and his faith in others' quick reaction times—leading him to the best decision within his understanding: attempting to cross the road. And then, in the blink of an eye, he was gone.

He is survived by his wife Carla and 3 children. Scott was an avid
runner and well-known competitor. He was known for his devotion
to his family and leadership in school and sports organizations,
where he impacted many lives.
— Obituary for Scott M. Birk

My Life

One of the obituaries for Scott mentioned that he was born and
raised in Wisconsin and attended Marquette University in Mil-
waukee. It noted, "Those who knew him will remember his warm
and caring spirit." His Midwestern roots resonated with me as that
warmth seemed to infuse every interaction I had with Scott. The
portrayal of his life by those who knew him left an impression on
me. I recall hoping my obituary would speak highly of me upon
my death but I feared it might be quite different.

Being from the Midwest myself, the obituary reminded me of
the rich context of my upbringing that I had seldom acknowledged.
The mention of Scott's hometown triggered thoughts of my own
hometown. I entered the world in South Bend, Indiana, in 1963;
within a year, my family moved to Brookville, Ohio. We lived a mere
stone's throw from my grandparents' home, where my father grew
up. It was also a short fifteen miles west of Dayton, my mother's
hometown. In my limited perspective, I thought everywhere
and every town resembled late 1960s Brookville—a tight-knit
community of around 3,200 people nestled amidst farmlands.
Here, a homogenous group of modest-income, frugal, faith-centered
Caucasians lived an unhurried life. It was a genuinely pleasant
place to call home.

As an adult, I came to cherish being recognized as a Midwesterner. I embraced the archetype of a Midwesterner, characterized
by inherent optimism, happiness, and a knack for putting smiles
on the faces of both friends and strangers that we meet.

Growing up, there were guidelines for nurturing God-fearing
children. My father instilled values of honesty, trustworthiness,

and dedication. However, as I matured, I grappled with the contrast between who I aspired to be and the person I truly was: a lonely and unhappy child at times.

Although I achieved milestones as an adult that many value—marriage to a hometown girl, a successful career, and three wonderful children—at some point, I could no longer escape the question: Was I ever genuinely happy? My outward accomplishments aside, I lived with an underlying unease. While I cherished my children and their ability to bring joy into my life, many of my days as a husband and a father were rote and unfulfilling. I felt affection for my former wife, but eventually acknowledged that I hadn't been in love with her for most of our marriage and that we had been staying married for our children's sake.

Despite achieving success in high-pressure sales jobs, the sales environment was one I despised. The demands of each job, the relentless pressure to meet quotas, and the inherent dissatisfaction I felt created a suffocating sense of stress which was a constant strain that weighed heavily on me. Each day seemed like a struggle, as the excitement of hitting sales targets one quarter faded in the face of new expectations the next. The rewards of reaching milestones, like prestigious awards and fabulous trips, were quickly overshadowed by the perpetual question, "What have you done lately?"

What I didn't know then is that I had never had a job that provided the emotional and personal satisfaction I sought. This was because there was a fundamental misalignment between my values and the work I was engaged in. Even the management track, which I initially thought would be more rewarding, presented its own set of challenges—particularly the gamut of personnel management concerns that arose alongside newfound authority.

I had pushed all these feelings aside so that they were barely perceptible, but once they rose to the surface, brought on in part by Scott Birk's death, my life began spiraling in ways I could not control. I began to question whether anyone truly has control.

Choices Made, Paths Taken

Throughout my upbringing, there were countless instances when I felt a lack of control: being told by my parents to do chores, not being picked for kickball, and experiencing a teenage breakup. As an adult, instances like a reckless driver on the freeway, a bar fight, or job loss due to a company division sale further underscored this sense of helplessness.

In the face of life's uncertainties, we often strive to regain control in any way possible. However, as I attempted to pinpoint the first time I took control in my life, my recollections of childhood failed to provide definitive answers. Reflecting on those seemingly pivotal choices, it became evident that the people around me exerted a significant influence.

Eating ice cream whenever I had the chance or forgetting the dreaded chore of taking out the trash hardly constituted control. Even asking a girl out during my teenage years, which seemed like a display of authority, was short-lived if she declined. The notion of control appeared again with decisions like choosing a college, opting for engineering, or applying to the University of Cincinnati (UC). At eighteen, legally an adult, I could do anything I wanted. However, my reasons for applying to UC over other, arguably more prestigious institutions like Harvard, Yale, or Oxford made me question the extent of control I truly exercised.

Like many American high school students, going to college was a given for me. It began during my freshman year of high school as an escape from my small hometown and to pave the way for a brighter future. However, not everyone I attended high school with had the same opportunities.

One of my friends, Jeff Schwartz, had been accepted by three Ohio universities and was interested in attending, but his lower high school GPA, lack of scholarships, and lack of parental support left him uncertain about paying for college. In search of alternatives, he considered joining the US Military. Jeff knew that the US Air Force regularly conducted the ASVAB (Armed Services Vocational

Aptitude Battery) admission test in Cincinnati, Ohio. Eager to move forward, one Saturday he took a Greyhound bus to Cincinnati and completed the test. After speaking with a few disinterested recruiters, Jeff returned to Dayton later that day. As he was walking to his car, he passed an open door and heard his nickname, "Hey, Red!" Startled, he looked around and noticed a US Marine Corps recruiter at a desk. The recruiter's attempt to catch Jeff's attention worked, leading Jeff to walk into the Marine Recruiting Office. The recruiter pointed to a poster depicting Marine recruits in training at boot camp and asked, "Think you can handle that?" With all the bravado he could muster, Jeff enthusiastically exclaimed, "Hell yes." In less than an hour, he had signed the initial paperwork to join the Marine Corps. The Marines offered Jeff the structure, plan, and compensation he wanted, providing him with the best path forward after high school.

Jeff and I deliberated over this scenario and concluded that the US Marine Corps recruiter likely exploited the vulnerability of individuals in transitional moments. With Dayton and Cincinnati in close proximity, the recruiters were well aware of the ASVAB test dates. The recruiting office's strategic proximity to the bus station and their knowledge of returning buses from Cincinnati meant that Jeff, among other Air Force candidates, was an accessible target. Jeff's response was stirred by both the attention and the allure of the challenge.

Not everyone is interested in pursuing higher education after high school. Another friend, Ronnie Loughman, disliked the homework load of high school, making college an unattractive option for him. He held various jobs until a family member told him about an opening at a company that serviced truck and trailer tires in Dayton, Ohio. Ronnie applied and got the job; however, after a few unsatisfying years, he realized he didn't want to be changing tires for the rest of his life. His exposure to truck drivers through his job led him to consider a new path. Becoming a truck driver offered better pay and the opportunity to travel. Ronnie dedicated himself to studying and practicing, ultimately passing his test for a commercial driver's license (CDL) to operate tractor-trailers. Recognizing this as his best chance, he made the decision to pursue this opportunity.

Three of us—Jeff, Ronnie, and myself—shared similar childhood experiences. However, we chose drastically different paths shaped by our individual histories. Yet, how many of these paths were truly the result of free will?

Control

While few believe they possess absolute control over every aspect of their lives, many hold onto the notion that there comes a point when we take control over our destinies and decisions. I had no say in my parents meeting, my birth itself, or my genetic makeup. Post-birth, I had no influence over the language I learned or the socioeconomic status of my family. So, when did I gain control?

Among my circle of friends and colleagues, most feel that the first time they were in control over their lives was when they selected a post-secondary school. Many among them applied to varying numbers of universities and received acceptances from a subset of these institutions. Conversations about college often include statements like, "I chose to attend Vanderbilt." However, when I inquire further by asking why they didn't opt for Harvard, the response often takes the form of, "How could I have chosen Harvard? I wasn't accepted!" This highlights a subtle distinction regarding choice—the unavailability of Harvard as an option meant it couldn't be "chosen." The illusion of "choice" is influenced by an array of countless factors.

Situations where individuals believe they exhibit control include:

- Refusing to eat.
- Skipping classes.
- Selecting a life partner.
- Picking a career path.
- Acquiring a vehicle.
- Accepting a job offer.

- Opting for a two-bedroom home priced at $160,000 over a five-bedroom home priced at $900,000.

These realms of presumed "control" revolve around three domains: the body, the mind, and the environment.

Controlling the body: You have the sensation of controlling your body when you move your arms and legs or run across a room. While you can make choices about what to eat to some extent, your body's hunger drives you to eat. Yet, there are body movements that seem initially under your control, like blinking, yawning, shivering, breathing, scratching, and laughing. However, these actions can often be triggered by internal and external stimuli beyond your direct control. This raises questions about the extent of your control over your body.

Control of the Mind: The feeling of controlling your mind appears when you decide what to think about. However, your mood, for instance, can be influenced by external events or chemical imbalances, impacting feelings of happiness or sadness. Hormones like dopamine link to pleasure, serotonin relates to memory, and norepinephrine, like adrenaline, governs stress and anxiety. Motivation, while something you can encourage, is often driven by external factors like deadlines or rewards. Finally, decision-making, despite being conscious, is often shaped by past experiences, biases, and emotions. The same applies to memory recall, creativity, and maintaining focus.

Control of the environment. Controlling our environment is a nuanced concept. We can have some influence on our surroundings, but external factors like weather, natural disasters, and societal structures often challenge our perception of control. This misconception often arises from our ability to observe patterns and make predictions. When these predictions align closely with actual outcomes, it reinforces the illusion of control. For instance, I once believed I had control in my former marriage because I accurately predicted that helping with childcare, occasionally cooking, and maintaining the house would make my former wife happy. However, it became evident that I couldn't control the fate of the relationship, as it was ultimately influenced by her independent feelings and decisions.

When something unexpected happens, the mind often engages in a process of cognitive recalibration to maintain a sense of control. It tries to make sense of the situation and does so by creating a narrative that aligns with the belief of having control. It tends to attribute outcomes to itself with bias, and it reframes unexpected events as temporary setbacks that, with enough willpower, can be overcome. Sometimes, the new reality is accompanied by an undeniable realization: maybe I am not in as much control as I thought.

Scott Birk likely believed he had control over his life's choices. He applied to Marquette University, got accepted, pursued his studies, graduated, and even took up running. It's probable that he felt in command on the day of the accident, choosing to run along the neighborhood streets and deciding to cross FM 2222. Yet, in an instant, factors beyond his control dramatically altered his reality. This raises a pertinent question: How does one lose control when confronted with unforeseen circumstances?

The notion of control must be straightforward. Either we have it, or we don't. However, many individuals believe and consciously accept the idea that control exists in varying degrees. They believe we have control over certain aspects like what we eat, our friends, our choice of life partners, or even the decision to read this book. Simultaneously, they accept a separate category where control lies in the hands of others, such as the notorious bumper-to-bumper traffic on Southern California's 405 freeway or my decision to write this book. Lastly, there's a third category which includes things that no one can control—physical laws like gravity, the rotation of the sun, or the weather. It's common for people to believe they have control while not giving a second thought to instances when they do not.

Countless events happen around me all the time. However, my body's senses can only capture a fraction of this reality, and my busy mind can only attend to a handful of these sensory inputs. As such, I cannot dismiss the idea that **control may simply be a persistent illusion due to my limited, unique view of reality.** Typically, we become aware of the lack of control when a sudden change occurs within our bodies, minds, or surroundings.

Do we only become aware of our lack of control when it leads to discomfort or harm? Consider this: when a joke triggers laughter, or a touching wedding moment brings tears to our eyes, we rarely dwell on the fact that these are also instances of losing control. It's a different matter, though, when laughter leads to an embarrassing incident, like wetting one's pants. Suddenly, the loss of control shifts from amusing to mortifying. Similarly, losing one's temper in traffic evokes a different reaction compared to shedding tears at a wedding. It appears my attitude toward control is inconsistent, swayed by the context of the experience. Positive experiences make me overlook, even enjoy, the relinquishing of control. In contrast, negative situations often leave me upset, sometimes repulsed, followed by regret and resentment once the initial emotional storm passes. This introspection led me to an intriguing realization: my sense of control, or the lack thereof, never really changes. It's driven by the fluctuating chemicals in my body, influencing my emotions. Logic suggests that to be truly in control, one must always be in control, but is this even possible for us as humans?

Building on this premise, if I am in control and then lose it, the cause must result from factors beyond my control. If I am truly in complete control, nothing should be able to trigger a loss of control. Therefore, I come to a compelling realization: if I have ever experienced a loss of control, it suggests that **I never truly possessed control in the first place**.

Living a life without control might seem frightening or even futile. However, if this is the truth of our existence, we are better off acknowledging that truth. Such awareness profoundly shapes us and grants context to comprehend the why and how of events, as well as highlights the significance of influence in our lives. This understanding relieves pressure, aids in avoiding negative influences when possible, and helps us recognize positive relationships and experiences that lead to a better, happier life.

The Year Before Scott's Death

During 2010, I held a high-pressure position as the senior vice president of sales and marketing for a Germany-based company. The role required frequent travel across the US for internal and customer meetings. Moreover, global leadership events mandated international travel for at least a week, taking me away from my family. Balancing executive responsibilities and personal challenges made 2010 an exceptionally demanding year for me. Despite achieving professional success, I was deeply unhappy. After more than a decade of marriage, my former wife and I found ourselves growing distant and decided to seek relationship counseling. To reduce pressure and distractions, our therapist suggested various strategies, one of which was taking up writing. The writing task was open-ended and lacked a specific topic or focus; it was more of a diversion. However, if we found it helpful or therapeutic, that would be an added benefit. Perhaps the act of writing aimlessly would provide us with some valuable introspection.

One Saturday morning, while sipping my morning coffee, I decided to give it a try. Initially, I saw it as a mindless activity, unaware that my storyline would mirror the love and relationship challenges I was facing in real life. As I delved into writing, I found myself documenting my emotional voyage, uncovering previously unknown facets of my relationships, and answering my own questions.

Throughout my life, I have read numerous books, both science fiction and nonfiction. My fascination with science fiction began when I read *A Wrinkle in Time* by Madeleine L'Engle, published in 1962. The imaginative tales transported me to worlds where fantastical events took place, which resonated deeply with my desires. Science fiction presented exciting possibilities, often interwoven with advanced technology, alternate realities, and far-reaching parts of the universe. These stories expanded my mind and gave me a sense that anything was possible.

One notable science-based book was Stephen Hawking's *A Brief History of Time*, published in 1988. The book, presenting modern physics in an accessible manner, fascinated me with its introduction to concepts like black holes. I was captivated by the idea that gravity in a black hole is so intense that nothing, not even light, can escape. This concept lingered in my mind for years. The notion that gravity could affect massless photons, despite their speed, intrigued me. My curiosity about these ideas led me to speculate: if the universe operates at the speed of light, then perhaps an object's mass determines its speed, giving rise to our perception of time. This line of thinking led me to imagine a universe without mass, possibly in another dimension, where time is experienced differently than in our own.

These thoughts gave birth to my manuscript, "No Time," a story set in a time-free universe. The protagonists, Jax and Dagny Montgomery, a father-daughter science team, embark on an energy experiment gone awry. This experiment results in a cataclysmic explosion, tearing their universe apart and birthing a white hole that triggers the Big Bang in our universe.

Developing the "No Time" narrative required extensive research in physics, philosophy, and cause-and-effect relationships to craft a conceivable world-universe model. This endeavor was time-consuming and distracting, leading me down a path of self-discovery, and prompting me to explore profound questions about my own existence, control, and responsibility.

Accidental Motivation: The Book

Although I enjoyed developing my "No Time" story idea, my mind drifted toward the looming question of whether or not we have any control. I started working on a manuscript that developed into *Accidental Motivation*, a vehicle to untangle the sprawling question, "What aspects of my life can I truly control?" Although my engineering background equipped me with analytical skills, the nature of control required deeper philosophical scrutiny. Complex questions about the Big Bang, the tug-of-war between evolution and creationism, moral relativism, and causality in a four-dimensional universe came into play. A simple scientific viewpoint couldn't resolve these intricacies thus when science fell short in offering answers, I delved into philosophy.

Additionally, my family life was falling apart and the ultimate question of who would be the first to break loomed large. I realized if I couldn't find my own happiness, the odds of my actions, love, and presence creating happiness for others were not good. My personal worldview needed some significant adjustments before I could project it outward. To that extent, I felt a sense of control.

On a memorable evening, December 9, 2013, I found myself amidst a group of fifteen intellectual seekers, gathered in a secluded dining area at La Madeleine in Austin. It was the Austin Philosophy Discussion Group (APDG) Meetup group meeting entitled "Contemporary Philosophy, Analytic Philosophy." They decided to present and discuss an overview of Analytic Philosophy, looking at three philosophers over three meetings: Gottlob Frege, Bertrand Russell, and Ludwig Wittgenstein. The meeting roster included a variety of keen minds. From my notes, attendees included Leonard Hough (host), Barbara, Hillary, Ronnie, Gary P., Bill Meacham (author and philosopher), Larry Yogman, Katherine (worked on a Frege paper in college), Philip Watts, Terry Ellis, Bene, Doshan, Guy Johnson, and Jack Hohengarten. For two hours, the group delved into the work of Frege, who was instrumental in shaping modern logic and analytic philosophy. Captivated by the scope of ideas, I felt alive in a way I hadn't in years. I made it a habit to jot down notes on my iPhone, using it as a repository for a plethora of concepts discussed, which I referred to frequently and as I began to open my mind and look at my life and the world differently.

That night was a significant moment for me. My curiosity grew and I became eager to learn more. Web browsing turned into a marathon of academic discovery as I waded through an ocean of philosophies, theories, and viewpoints. Even as questions remained unresolved, new ones cropped up—like the eternal debate over objective good and bad, or the societal contracts we might be bound to from birth.

Thoughts about Scott Birk's tragic accident frequently resurfaced for me. His untimely, uncontrollable death served as a haunting reminder of life's unpredictability. If anything had been different, Scott would be alive. But nothing could be different. Even the most prominent runner among us was not immune to fate's whims. If it could happen to him, it could happen to anyone, including me.

In a world where the illusion of having control can potentially be as dangerous as the belief that we have no control, it begs the question: When does our quest for control become futile? If random events can upend lives regardless of our perceived control over our lives, relationships, and decisions, what then is the true goal of our existence? More important, do we have any influence? How can we use our limited sphere of influence to our advantage?

CHASING HAPPINESS

"Happiness is the meaning and the purpose of life: the whole aim and end of human existence."
— Aristotle

My Childhood

Born in South Bend, Indiana, I was moved to Ohio at the age of two, making it an integral part of my life. The history lessons from my primary education in Ohio were often dull and I struggled to remember dates and events that had no personal relevance to me. However, some facts remained etched in my memory, while others faded over time. I recalled Ohio's statehood in 1803, its place as the seventeenth state of the Union, and its approximate 5.4 percent share of the U.S. population in 1960. Everything beyond Ohio in 1803 was the Wild West—a vast frontier encompassing the Louisiana Territory (France), the Viceroyalty of New Spain (Spain), and the unclaimed northwest territory. Modern Ohio held its share of remarkable moments. In 1962, Ohioan John Glenn became the first person to orbit the Earth. In 1963, the Pro Football Hall of Fame opened in Canton, Ohio. Most notably, in 1969, fellow Ohioan Neil Armstrong became the first human to set foot on the moon.

Despite the claustrophobia my hometown would eventually represent to me, it was a wonderful place to grow up, full of genuine Midwesterners.

My father, Kenneth Leroy Holsinger, was born in 1938, the eldest of four siblings. In rural Ohio, opportunities for learning were limited to family, church, and school. He taught himself the trombone and played in school bands. He also joined Brookville Boy Scout Troop 47, founded in 1917 and one of the oldest troops in the U.S. In July 1953, he attended the National Scout Jamboree in California and was involved for many years with the Dayton YMCA.

After high school, he pursued his passion for music and explored life beyond Ohio by joining the U.S. Air Force Band. His enlistment was cut short due to a heart condition, leading to an honorable discharge. Back in Ohio, he took a job with Allied/Egry Business Systems, met my mother, Theresa Berkemeier, and got married. Just five months after their wedding, my older sister arrived and in November 1963, I was born, followed by two more siblings eight and ten years later.

My early childhood was joyful and uneventful. I felt no responsibilities and often entertained myself when I was very young. I have cherished memories of long sunny summer days playing outside until it got dark. I would feel a sense of sadness when we were called inside for dinner or bedtime, signaling the end of those enjoyable Midwestern days.

Each summer since 1951, our town held the Brookville Community Picnic at Golden Gate Park—a three-day celebration featuring games, watermelon-eating contests, carnival rides, cotton candy, sugar waffles, music, and entertainment. It was where I witnessed a steam tractor powering a sawmill for the first time. The Brookville Picnic was the highlight of my year, only surpassed by Christmas.

At the start of each school year, my mother would take me to a Dayton Sears store to buy one pair of Lee or Levi's denim jeans. I distinctly remember beginning school with a stiff, deep blue pair of jeans. By year-end, they would be comfortable, faded, and often patched. My wardrobe consisted of one pair of jeans, a few short and long-sleeved shirts, and Keds gym shoes. Despite our modest socioeconomic status, there was no sense of discontent. I never felt poor or disadvantaged, and this sentiment was shared by others in town. The sense of equality prevailed; I never envied what others had or felt lesser due to my clothing or where I lived.

Occasionally, I'd ask for something frivolous like Coca-Cola, but the response was always, 'We don't have the money for that.' It was true; I don't remember feeling bothered by my situation, but I do remember feeling a desire for something different, something better than what I had experienced up to that point.

Preadolescent Influence – Mr. Peanut's Guide to Physical Fitness

In small-town America during the 1960s and 1970s, opportunities for sustained engagement for children were scarce unless they lived on farms or were required to work. Seasonal activities like Pee Wee (Pop Warner) football in the fall and Little League baseball in the summer, along with Scouting programs, provided avenues for involvement. Golden Gate Park in Brookville featured group shelters, a dance hall, swings, seesaws, and a baseball field. On the rare summer nights when my mother took us there, it felt like a carnival. The bustling scene involved playing with numerous friends, watching softball games, drinking Coca-Cola, and enjoying flat taffy chilled in an icebox

In my neighborhood, we often played freeze tag, tackle the runner, and hide and seek. As one of the younger kids, being easily caught didn't bother me—I was happy to be part of the fun. However, it wasn't until Mr. Peanut emerged as a fitness icon in 1970 that I became keenly aware of my physical fitness.

In 1966, President Lyndon B. Johnson established the Presidential Physical Fitness Award, recognizing school-aged children in the top fifteenth percentile across seven physical fitness tests. This initiative later became the President's Challenge Youth Physical Fitness Awards Program.

Planters Nut & Chocolate Company introduced the character Mr. Peanut in 1916, and after the company was acquired by Standard

Brands in 1960, efforts to enhance brand recognition through advertising gained momentum. In 1967, Mr. Peanut assumed the role of a 'Health Expert,' positioned as a fitness advisor by proclaiming, "Peanuts grow too, a lot like boys and girls. And Mr. Peanut knows all about growing big and strong." This set the stage for his fitness guidance.

I learned about Mr. Peanut's Guide to Physical Fitness during my Westbrook Elementary School's Physical Education class. Geared toward kids aged seven through nine, this fitness program revolved around seven activities: flexed arm hang; trunk flexion; sixty-second sit-ups; standing broad jump; fifty-yard dash; softball throw; and 600-yard run-walk. These exercises were unfamiliar to most of us, but we gathered with animated enthusiasm as each was explained.

During the 600-yard run-walk, our Physical Education teacher, Mr. Kinsel, instructed everyone to line up behind me on the track. With little explanation, we were directed to jog around the track. When someone tried to pass me, I shouted that Mr. Kinsel wanted me to be the leader, and to stay behind me. Leading the class across the finish line filled me with joy, but Mr. Kinsel noted our slow pace, which left me puzzled because he had not said anything about performing the run-walk quickly. We completed the run with a time over three minutes, and everyone in the class earned a BRONZE achievement.

The excitement carried through the various tests, but anxiety grew as my results were noted on the *Official Mr. Peanut Certificate*. Dread set in. I didn't understand "Trunk Flexion" and couldn't touch my toes, let alone reach eleven inches below them for a GOLD rating. My "Flexed Arm Hang" barely lasted a second before turning into a straight arm hang and quickly ending with me dropping to the floor.

Watching other boys effortlessly throw a softball amazed me. They seemed expert in winding up and launching the ball. I eagerly awaited my turn. "Stand a few feet behind the starting line. Move up and throw the ball overhand as far as you can," said Mr. Kinsel.

Bending down, I grabbed the hefty softball, struggling to balance it in one hand. Lifting it above my shoulder, I ran forward and threw it with all my strength. To my confusion, the ball bounced and stopped before reaching the pitcher's mound, just sixty feet away. Laughter echoed around me, and that moment of embarrassment has remained etched in my memory. I never threw another softball.

I consistently performed at the lowest level on all the Mr. Peanut exercises, earning the designation of BRONZE, which indicated "Needs Improvement." However, this assessment of my physical performance didn't motivate me; it brought stress and lingering discomfort that lasted longer than it should have. I was being judged on activities that were totally unfamiliar to me, showcasing my shortcomings in front of my peers. Whether this experience fueled a desire to overcome my physical limitations in adulthood remains uncertain, but it did bring a significant sense of sadness in the moment. These tests, my subsequent lackluster performance, and the results documented on a certificate for my parents were sources of embarrassment and a burden that stayed with me for many years.

WHILE RESEARCHING MR. PEANUT, I stumbled upon an old pamphlet titled 'Mr. Peanut's Guide to Physical Fitness.' What caught my eye was the introduction written by Dr. Paul Hunsicker, a chairman at the University of Michigan and a notable expert in physical education during his time. Despite his credentials, his introduction reveals a lot about the prevailing societal attitudes back then, some of which now seem woefully out of touch.

The introduction on the inside of the front cover read as follows:

TO TEACHERS AND PARENTS—
Physical fitness is important for everyone. Like most good habits,
the pattern should be set at an early age. The elementary school
teacher can help by promoting activities that will make young
people aware of the need for good fitness practices. Parents can

help by encouraging their youngsters and approving their physical fitness activities.

Youngsters and adults alike should recognize the importance of exercise for the healthy growth and development needed to cope with today's busy and challenging times. Good exercise practices need to be carried out regularly so that fitness is maintained from one year to the next.

Boys need to be physically fit so that they can compete in sports and later can compete in society. Girls need to be physically fit because it makes them more attractive.

Pupils using this book of physical fitness should compare their test scores with those of previous performances. Without exception, improvement is usually possible for all pupils.

—Paul Hunsicker[1]

He notes that boys should strive for physical fitness to compete in society, while girls should do so merely to enhance their attractiveness. These views, while perhaps accepted in that era, stand as stark reminders of how much we've evolved—and how even the most well-regarded experts can be products of their time, shaped by the prejudices and limitations of their society.

By sharing this, I'm not only reflecting on how far we've come but also am reminded that our current knowledge and attitudes will one day be scrutinized by future generations. It serves as a humbling call to always question the norms that surround us and to strive for greater understanding.

Iron Eyes Cody and Ecology

In the 1970s, during a time when President Johnson's push for improved fitness was in full swing, the environmental movement was also gaining momentum, advocating for cleaner air and water. This era saw the iconic "Crying Indian" public service announcement, a poignant campaign launched by Keep America Beautiful and the Ad Council in 1971. As a seven-year-old, I vividly remember the stirring image of Iron Eyes Cody, an actor portraying a Native American, in this ad that debuted on Earth Day.

The ad showed Cody paddling down a polluted river, passing smog-emitting factories, and standing near a littered highway. The defining moment came when a bag of trash thrown from a car lands at his feet, and a single tear rolls down his cheek as a narrator solemnly states, "People start pollution. People can stop it." This powerful message resonated nationwide, emphasizing the environmental consequences of our actions.

Around this time, I joined the Boy Scouts of America (BSA), an organization deeply rooted in outdoor ethics and conservation. Being part of the BSA during this environmentally conscious era meant that our activities often echoed the growing concern for our planet. I was a Bear Scout in third grade and we took on an environmentally-focused project.

However, coming from a family with limited means, accessing the necessary tools and materials for my original project idea proved difficult. Resourcefully, my mother suggested an alternative: baking and decorating a cake with an environmental theme. Inspired by the commercials and messages I had seen, including the memorable "Crying Indian" ad, I wanted to incorporate the ecology symbol into my project.

Living in a small Ohio town in the 1970s meant that finding information beyond what was taught at school was quite a challenge. We primarily relied on newspapers, evening TV news broadcasts, and a treasured set of the Encyclopedia Britannica, which my mother had bought from a door-to-door salesman. Each volume in this set was numbered and covered topics in alphabetical order, ranging from Volume 1 'A to ANNO' to Volume 23 'VASE to ZYGO,' and was updated annually with a 'Book of the Year.' Despite my best efforts scouring Volume 7, 'DAMASCU to EDUC,' for information on 'Ecology,' I couldn't find the symbol I remembered. Due to our limited resources, we had to be creative; we ended up decorating our cake with the word 'ECOLOGY' in red icing, a stark contrast to the green circular symbol that adorned the projects of many other Scouts.

This experience was a lesson in how our access to knowledge is shaped by our immediate environment and resources. It showed me that our understanding of the world is often limited to what those around us know and what information we can access. The "Crying Indian" campaign and my time in the Scouting programs highlighted the importance of environmental awareness, but also the challenges faced when resources are scarce.

1974 – The Year of Loss

In 1974, my father's last job was working as a car salesman at Westbrook Dodge, a local car dealership. I remember the day we picked up our used 1972 Ford Country Squire station wagon. I was excited to claim the back seat and its unique rear-facing third row. The novelty of this carnival-like feature allowed me to see the world from the rear window. At the time, we were unaware that this station wagon design would later be associated with tragic carbon monoxide poisoning, caused by exhaust gases entering the vehicle through the lowered rear gate window. But our family's experience with death took a different form.

During that same year, my father experienced sudden weight gain and fatigue. He was immediately referred to a heart specialist at Wright Patterson Air Force Base, forty minutes away. The diagnosis was congestive heart failure, a condition that weakens the heart's ability to pump blood effectively. With limited options, he faced open-heart surgery for a mechanical heart valve replacement.

A snapshot of our family standing in front of our home the day my father left for the hospital captures a moment forever etched in my memory. In hindsight, the reason for this photo became clear— his health, and his survival, was uncertain. Little did I know then the significance of that image or the emotions it would evoke. My parents flew to San Antonio, Texas, for his surgery in September

1974. They returned within a couple weeks but unfortunately, my memories from that time are limited and negative. I recall the sadness I felt seeing my father lying in bed and my callous reaction to an awful meal we had after they returned because my mother had eliminated salt due to my father's dietary restriction. His condition worsened over time; he was bedridden and weakening. After six weeks, doctors discovered that his mechanical valve was leaking.

As my parents prepared to leave for the airport to fly to San Antonio a second time, my mother took me aside and said, "Hug your father. You are staying with your Uncle Doug this weekend." That turned out to be the last time I saw him alive. His body couldn't handle the stress of post-surgery recovery, and his heart stopped. Uncle Doug, my father's only brother, delivered the heartbreaking news. It was an unexpected shock, and tears flowed as I struggled to grasp the idea of life without my father. I wondered, who would be there for my basketball games?

Time passed slowly in my uncle's arms as my mind raced through selfish concerns. Then, a phone call pierced the silence. Uncle Doug left for a moment and returned with astounding news; two phone calls, ten minutes apart, took me from the depths of despair to my first peak experience—he's gone, no, wait, your prayers have been answered, he's alive. Thanks be to God.

A few days later, my siblings and I returned home to my grandmother's care while my parents were still in Texas. One evening, Mimi entered my room, hugged me tightly, and delivered the same dreadful news again: my father had passed away. I sat on the bed in shock without shedding a tear. The recurring thought echoed: Who would be there to watch my games? In time, I connected this concern to a universal need for validation. Who would witness my achievements, my performances, and tell me I had succeeded?

Ken Holsinger passed away on November 11, 1974, at just thirty-six years old. The turmoil from this loss was profound, but what stands out in my memory are the reactions of those around us. Family and friends consoled me with words like, "sometimes

God takes the good ones." While well-intentioned, this was hard to accept. It seemed to suggest that my father's death was an exception to the notion that good people should have longer lives. Why would God take my father if he was good?

Over time, I realized I had two choices: either God was cruel, or his body had naturally deteriorated. I later learned it began with rheumatoid fever contracted in the military, which led to irreparable heart damage. Either way, his death was beyond his control and mine. At ten years old, grappling with this truth was unsettling. As a child, it hurt to think that God, with a snap of his fingers, could have spared him. Yet, in the grand scheme, medical science at that time could not have prevented his passing; the forces of nature were in control.

Religious Influence

Religion played a significant role in my upbringing, with both my parents having different faiths—my father Methodist, my mother Catholic. We were raised Catholic, attending mass every weekend and receiving religious instruction (Catechism) on Wednesdays. Instead of my parents creating their own moral code to guide their actions and decisions, religion provided their moral values. It was a ready-made framework that shaped their understanding of right and wrong.

I was a well-behaved child, not because I cared about doing what was right, but because I was driven by a fear of a punishing God who had the power to condemn people to hell for any number of reasons. One of the most terrifying was the idea of dying with original sin, something only baptism and God's forgiveness could cleanse. I couldn't help but worry about the fate of babies who died shortly after birth, potentially facing damnation. Despite being baptized myself, I still harbored a deep fear of going to hell. I even wore the Brown Scapular, a cloth medal believed to offer protection from eternal damnation. Additionally, I had been led to believe that God had taken my father for reasons beyond our understanding, which led to even more questions. Whenever I sought answers, I was often met with responses like, "You shouldn't ask why; you should be asking what you can do and turn to God for answers." But there were no answers, of course, which only left me yearning to understand the 'why' behind it all.

The loss of such an important person was unmistakable, and the fact that my father was a good person, in my estimation, made it difficult to grasp why God would take him away. I applied simple logic: do good deeds, receive rewards; do bad things, face consequences. Statements like "we can't understand God's actions, but trust and believe in Him" pushed me away from religion.

Even before I became an adult, I began to question the fear-driven religious beliefs that my family had instilled in me. While I loved my parents and believed they had good intentions, they simply passed down what they were taught. It's unfortunate that fear controlled me for so long. Afterlife and heaven couldn't be proven or disproven and I struggled to reconcile the cognitive dissonance created by the realities of my life. Eventually, I began to deconstruct these beliefs and distance myself from the burden of fearing God in my pursuit of happiness, but it took years to let go of the unnecessary guilt that burdened me, making me feel responsible and unfairly treated by God. My father's passing had a profound impact on me, shaping the way I behaved and was a trigger for many of my teenage choices. Three years after my father died, I played basketball with only my mother watching from the bleachers.

A Mother's Struggles

When my mother was a child, the conventional American family structure consisted of two married individuals. My mother grew up in a household where mid-century American values prevailed, along with distinct family roles, a God-centric faith, discipline, and gender-specific rules. Her father, August John Berkemeier, supported the family financially, set the rules, and took on the role of disciplinarian. On the other hand, her mother, Edith "Mimi" (Mauchamer) Berkemeier, tended to the children, managed household duties, and cooked. My mother learned her place within this family dynamic, modeling herself after my beloved grandmother. She mastered her role, yet it didn't encompass the dual responsibilities of being both mother and father after my father's passing.

During the summer of 1975, as I prepared to enter middle school, my family was still adjusting to our new home and the absence of my father. My mother didn't have a full-time job, and her idle time made it challenging to adapt to life without her husband. We had moved to a new house less than a month after my father's death and it's possible my parents realized the uncertainty of my father's health and planned accordingly. Whatever the plan, my mother struggled to support a family of four on government assistance and below-poverty-level wages. The years following my father's death were difficult and turned our once happy and stable family into a sad and fearful one.

Some nights, my older sister and I stayed up late watching television with my mother until the broadcasts went off the air for the night. On many occasions, she allowed us to sleep with her in her bed—an unusual occurrence when my father was alive. Though it was fun for all of us, I now realize she must have been hiding almost unbearable sadness. My mother bore all the responsibility for keeping four children aged four to fourteen healthy. The year after his passing was undeniably the most challenging of her life. It's difficult to fathom the loneliness and depression she must have faced. She took odd jobs to make ends meet—selling Avon, working at a soda shop, and eventually at our town's video store. Understandably, my older sister and I took on additional chores and assumed expanded responsibilities for our younger siblings. We carried out our greater responsibilities with almost no supervision.

Before we could mark the first anniversary of my father's passing, our lives were shaken once again by my mother's diagnosis with breast cancer. At eleven years old, I couldn't fully grasp the gravity of the situation, but I understood that it was bad news. The only treatment option was a total mastectomy, involving the removal of the entire breast, chest muscle lining, and some lymph nodes in the underarm area. Unbeknownst to me, her life was in danger, and the pain our family was experiencing was on the verge of intensifying tenfold. Looking back, I now understand that her death would have irreparably shattered me and my siblings.

I watched as my mother stood in the kitchen, inching her right hand up the wall as a form of therapy. As she reached her limit for the day, a wince of pain crossed her face. Unaware of the extent of her physical challenges, I sat at the kitchen table eating lunch, puzzled by her seemingly odd behavior of staring at the wall while moving her hand upward.

Sometime later, she showed us the prosthesis that fit inside her bra. I responded with disgust, wondering why she had to show it to me. In hindsight, it's evident that she had few, if any, individuals with whom she could share the challenges she faced. As kids, we were alive and had no understanding that our life as a family was so fragile.

Later that same year, I entered the sixth grade with my father gone and my mother's health stabilizing, but I felt lost. Today, I might be labeled as depressed or anxious, yet back then, I was simply "a troubled youth." I gained weight, missed seventeen school days, and just managed to scrape by with my grades. My teacher, Ms. Ozimek, understood my situation. She accommodated my absences, offering support and encouragement during one of my most difficult years.

Little did we know, my mother was living day by day, grappling with the fear of her cancer recurring. Fortunately, she survived and never experienced a cancer recurrence. When I was diagnosed with melanoma in 2007, I gained a profound understanding of her situation. Over the years, the realization of nearly losing her fostered in me a deep appreciation for her role as both mother and father in our family. Her worries about cancer added to the challenges of raising us four kids. It took years of being cancer-free before she

could truly relax, knowing she had triumphed over cancer and successfully raised a family despite numerous obstacles. I'm certain that
in her mind, she felt that God had tested her in countless, nearly
insurmountable ways, but her dedication to family and faith had
ultimately prevailed. She was a truly good and moral person, and
her strength carried her through the most difficult moments.

The Phone Repair Adventure of '76

During the summer of 1976, our phone service at home was disrupted by ongoing construction in a neighboring lot. My mother
reported the issue to the phone company, who scheduled a repair
for seven days later. During that time, I found myself drawn to
the excavated area as a source of novelty, providing a welcome
break from my usual boredom and a rare chance to stumble upon
something more intriguing than watching TV.

Scaling a small mound of dirt, I spotted a hole in the ground
likely left by the backhoe's work the previous day. The hole was a
couple of feet wide, and a single underground telephone cable had
been split, leaving four color-coded wires exposed and dangling at
each end. I quickly recognized that the situation presented me with
an opportunity to find a makeshift solution to our phone service
problem before the professional repairman arrived at our house.

The cable had snapped, leaving the copper wires barely protected
by their insulation. I needed a tool to cut the casing and reconnect the
wires. Remembering my father's toolbox, I ventured into the garage,
which was still cluttered with cardboard boxes from our move over
a year ago. I had to shift several stacked boxes to access the toolbox
nestled in a corner. After several exhausting minutes, I uncovered it.

The tools within the portable, rust-covered steel toolbox were
once off-limits when the toolbox rested on the wooden workbench
in our Ankara Avenue garage. The treasure trove, once forgotten
and gathering dust, was mine to plunder.

Upon opening the lid, I searched through the contents, finding
a hammer, a flat-head screwdriver (no extravagant Phillips one),

a pair of pliers, and a few unfamiliar tools. Yet, nothing suitable for cutting a wire. This marked the first of many instances in my early life when I lacked the right tool or fastener—a small nail for hanging a picture, the correct-sized wrench, the precise nut, bolt, or screw for school or home projects. I grew to despise such experiences, and when I could afford it later in life, I made Home Depot my Shangri-La, amassing every tool I might ever need.

Without a wire-cutting tool in sight, I tackled the problem in a way that would later prove to be an ongoing nuisance for my mother. I simply grabbed a sharp paring knife typically used for peeling apples and headed out with my makeshift splice tool. With unskilled hands, I stripped the wire insulation, matched the colors, and luckily had enough slack to join and twist the wires together. Uncertain if my repair would hold, I ran inside, lifted the telephone receiver, and heard a dial tone—a satisfying sense of achievement.

Post-repair, my concern shifted to the possibility of the exposed wires touching and causing a short circuit. Back to the toolbox, I fruitlessly hunted for a roll of black electrical tape. I sifted through our cluttered kitchen drawers, discovering only cellophane tape—unsuitable for the job due to rain risks. Then my gaze fell upon a box of birthday cake candles. Eureka! Armed with candles and my mother's shiny new BIC lighter, I returned to my project, lit a candle, and dripped wax around each wire splice. Stepping back, I admired my handiwork, reveling in the satisfaction of a job well done.

A week later, an Ohio Bell Telephone Company repairman arrived at our house. The repair proved straightforward, and once he finished, he knocked on our front door to ensure the phone was working. He asked who had performed the wire splicing, a mix of bemusement and curiosity in his expression. Cautiously, I admitted my involvement, unsure if I had done something wrong. When I told him how I protected the wires, a wide grin broke across his face. My ingenuity had clearly impressed him—at least, that's how I remember it, a proud child yearning for approval.

IN THE FALL OF 1976, as I began seventh grade, a remarkable transformation occurred: I underwent a growth spurt, shedding my baby weight and shooting up by a whopping seven inches. I immersed myself in sports, school activities, and my academic courses, resulting in a string of straight A grades. Yet, the real highlight came when my name appeared on the honor roll for the first time that fall. A note of congratulations from Ms. Ozimek filled me with an overwhelming sense of pride. My outlook on life changed, becoming considerably brighter than it had been in quite some time.

I also became interested in building Revell plastic model cars and painting them using Estes paints. However, my interests took an unexpected turn when an advertisement for a handheld electronic game caught my eye.

Determined to share my interest, I made it my mission to capture my mother's attention during commercials and by circling electronic games in the Sears catalog. My persistence paid off when I received a Mattel Electronics Auto Race game as a Christmas gift in 1976—this was one of the earliest handheld electronic games available. The following year, I got my hands on the next iteration of Mattel's handheld electronics, the awe-inspiring Mattel Football game. Growing up during the technological boom was exhilarating, as each passing year unveiled new and exciting innovations that I simply couldn't get enough of.

Fast forward three decades, and my five-year-old son was introduced to his first device: an Apple iPad, which made its debut on April 3, 2010.

Children of the Corn

In July of 1977, my mother signed me up for a farm job at Dull Homestead, the area's largest employer known for growing hybrid seed corn. The Dull farm specialized in producing hybrid seed corn through the cross-pollination of two pure genetic lines of corn.

On my first day, my mother dropped me off with a brown bag lunch and instructions to find Joy Dull. Joy handled scheduling, and from what I observed, ran the entire business from her farmhouse dining room table. A group of about forty kids gathered near the garage as Joy posted the crew assignment sheets. She told us to find our name and crew leader and join them at their trucks. I was excited but waited until the crowd thinned to move closer to the lists taped to the garage wall. There it was—my name written beneath the crew leader Ralph Dull. Ralph's crew was responsible for detasseling corn, which involved removing the pollen-producing tassel from each male row stalk to facilitate cross-pollination.

It came as no surprise that I didn't know Ralph, considering how large the Dull family was. I turned to a couple older kids and asked where I could find Ralph. Their eyes widened, and one of them smirked as he pointed towards a truck, saying, "That's Ralph, he's the owner, and the toughest crew leader out here."

I climbed into the back of Ralph's pickup truck, quietly keeping my head down as we traveled for half a mile. Our destination was a corn field where we would spend the entire day. Upon arrival, we hopped out of the truck and gathered at the edge of the corn field around Ralph. He asked if any of us were new to detasseling and a few hands, including mine, went into the air.

Ralph tutored us about the significance of tassels and ear shoots in corn plants. He explained that tassels represented the male flowers, while ear shoots represented the female flowers. Our responsibility entailed removing tassels from the female rows of corn to facilitate cross-pollination with the male rows. To demonstrate, Ralph grabbed the prominent yellow tassels at the top of a corn stalk and plucked them out. He told us if the tassel seemed hidden to gently grip the top of the stalk, rolling the leaves between our fingers, until we felt the tassel. Peeling back the leaves would allow easy removal of the tassel. Our responsibility was crystal clear: remove every single tassel without exception to prevent open pollination, which could lead to the contamination of hybrid seed.

Being a kid in a cornfield entrusted with such significant responsibility created an unprecedented level of focus within me. As

Ralph pulled the rope start on the detasseling machine's engine, I cautiously climbed aboard. This high-clearance tractor featured four suspended, two-person metal baskets. I spent eight hours in that basket, only taking a break for lunch, completely absorbed in a single row of green corn stalks flowering with bright yellow tassels.

Throughout the entire day, Ralph Dull's watchful eye remained on us, yet he never directly addressed me. He allowed me to tackle my task independently, and I kept to myself, fully engrossed in the most important job I had ever had. Despite the scorching summer sun, the day seemed to pass quickly. My fear of failure, coupled with my unwavering focus on detasseling each stalk, rendered me oblivious to everything else, including the passage of time.

Working with a crew of schoolmates on a farm in the middle of a cornfield was an exciting new experience, made even more so by my fear of Ralph, the quiet yet commanding patriarch of the Dull Homestead. The day was arduous and demanding. When my mother picked me up, her question "How was your day?" was met with a typical teenager's response: "Good, what's for dinner?" Later, exhaustion crept in, leading to an early bedtime. Early mornings were routine on the farm, and my efforts earned me another day of work.

The next morning, after my mother dropped me off, I stowed my lunch inside the garage and set out to find my crew assignment for the day. Joy, whom I discovered was Ralph's wife, posted the crew assignments. As I approached, she said, "You're on Ralph's crew again." My initial reaction was one of trepidation, but before I could react, she continued, "Ralph said you did a great job yesterday." While I heard the words, the magnitude of her comment escaped me. The combination of my apprehension toward Ralph and my fear of failure drove me to maintain focus and excel in my performance. My work stood out, and I was recognized for being an above average worker. Looking back, Joy's mention of Ralph's favorable feedback regarding my first day's work set me on a trajectory that would shape the course of my life.

In the summer of 1978, my second year on the farm, a new challenge emerged. I received a call to start working ahead of the others, assigned to a rogueing crew comprised of more experienced farm hands. The prospect was both exhilarating and daunting. On my first field day, our crew leader, Kevin Dull—Ralph's youngest son—explained our task and displayed an example of a rogue corn stalk. As we began hacking down the rogue corn, a sense of purpose welled up within me, as though I was part of something special.

My third year on the farm ushered in an unexpected promotion—a crew leader role, despite being among the youngest workers. The promotion wasn't entirely unexpected, given that the members of the rogueing crew were already recognized as valuable workers who set an example in the field. Many of them had also served as crew leaders during the detasseling process. Embracing my role as a crew leader, I relished the chance to operate the detasseling tractors—a thrilling experience. However, at that time, I hadn't fully grasped the significance of being in a leadership role. I was simply having fun, unaware that I was learning valuable leadership skills at such a young age.

During a scorching July day, I was leading a crew tasked with detasseling a cornfield running alongside Interstate 70. Mid-afternoon, I granted the crew a well-deserved break, reminding them to stay hydrated. What began as a standard water break turned into lighthearted amusement as we playfully waved cornstalks in the air, eliciting honks from passing cars on the highway. Some drivers responded, acknowledging the sight of kids on the edge of a cornfield.

During the break, Steve Staats, a larger worker, approached and, in a playful manner, hoisted me upside down in his arms. While it was all in good fun, I was surprised as he playfully shook me. Kevin Dull swiftly intervened, sternly telling Steve to put me down. In the summer of 2023, discussing this situation, Kevin said that he often enjoyed the hands-on detasseling work, even though it was uncommon for a crew leader to have a Dull family member in their crew. This was a refreshing change from his usual leadership duties.

While I held the title of crew leader that day, it was apparent that I hadn't yet earned the respect of everyone on my crew. Following the incident, Kevin pulled me aside, emphasizing the impropriety of the situation and urged me to assert control. With a chuckle and a slight shake of his head, he remarked, "And never let anyone turn you upside down again." This experience marked a pivotal moment in understanding leadership dynamics and having confidence in my own convictions.

The true impact of my time at the Dull Homestead farm crystallized six years later during an interview for an Industrial Engineer job with Huffy Bicycles, part of my college co-op program. One question caught me off guard: "You held a team leader role. Tell me about that." It hadn't crossed my mind that such an experience would be pertinent when applying for an engineering position. Within months, I joined Huffy Bicycles, where the hiring manager revealed that my resume stood out among fifteen applicants. The defining factor was my stint as a team leader detasseling corn at the Dull Homestead farm. The insight gained that day remained with me, underscoring how past experiences shape our futures—a valuable lesson I endeavored to impart to my children.

Influential Absence

Almost a year after my father's death, I experienced a dream which became a fond memory. In the dream, my father appeared at our doorstep. As you might imagine, seeing a loved one who had passed stirred up a whirlwind of emotions within me. The joy of talking with my father and asking him about his experiences has stayed with me for my entire life. Though I know it was a dream, the memory of the conversation is as real in my mind as any other memory. It's truly astonishing how our subconscious can craft such intricate experiences in our dreams, where the impossible seems possible. When I woke up, I was filled with excitement. The experience, crafted by my mind, flooded my body with endorphins, solidifying the dream in my memory forever. I have a tangible memory of an event that only happened within my brain that night—a conversation with my father—that was real to me, and I carry the associated emotions and memories with me to this day.

As I entered eighth grade in the fall of 1977, my father's absence weighed heavily on me, even though he had been gone for nearly three years. What remained were fond memories and an aching heart left by my dream. His influence came alive through stories of his youth as a musician and Boy Scout, and his later years in the military, serving his country while exploring the world. Inspired to follow in his footsteps, his absence served as the driving force behind my own personal growth.

And then there was my mother. A cheerful, warm, and loving woman who frequently welcomed extended family and friends into our home for shared meals, drinks, and card games. Alcohol was a constant presence, and she sometimes allowed people to spend the night due to overindulgence. She found ways to enjoy her friendships and create a lively and inviting atmosphere in our home. Whenever a knock sounded at our front door, I'd often hear queries like, "Is there a card game going on?", "What's for dinner?", or "I was passing by on I-70 and thought I'd drop in."

During my early teenage years, our home turned into a regular gathering place, exposing me to diverse people and ideas. In hindsight, I realize that this is where I cultivated my social skills and acceptance of others. I could connect with athletes or rednecks as easily as I could talk with the high school principal or the president of the School Board of Education. This flexibility served me well from working with my coworkers in Dull's cornfields to my colleagues at Huffy Bicycle. My appreciation for my mother's open-mindedness and non-judgmental nature remains strong, and I believe that these qualities persist in me today due to her influence.

She seemed to know everyone in Brookville and was well-versed in the town's happenings. This connectedness led to various odd job opportunities for me, aside from corn detasseling. Throughout my teen years, I mended severed telephone wires, patched drywall holes, painted walls, hung wallpaper, laid ceramic floor tiles, captured mice, and laid to rest many fish, parakeets, and dogs. I painted houses inside and out, installed residential vinyl siding, performed maintenance at a local nursing home, and worked on residential construction projects across Dayton. My teenage years were filled with long hours of hard work. Each challenge engaged my mind and provided a chance for self-education across a diverse array of subjects. However, with every job or chore, I knew that the most complex challenges facing my family such as my mother's depression, our financial struggles, and my sister's impulsive elopement at age sixteen were beyond my ability to address.

1978 – Hard work vs. Smart Work

My grandmother, Mimi, often spent weekends at our house, helping raise her grandchildren. Having been widowed a year before my birth, she understood the challenges my mother faced in raising four children aged six to fifteen. Mimi possessed an unwavering work ethic, was a wonderful cook, and prepared many of our weekend meals. She always radiated beauty and meticulousness in her appearance. It was during her visits that I came to understand that her meticulousness extended to maintaining household order and cleanliness. With four kids in the house during the week, chaos often reigned, and thus, under Mimi's guidance, every Saturday became a designated cleaning time.

The summer before my freshman year in high school, Mimi handed me a specific task: thoroughly clean the kitchen floor. Our kitchen boasted a 1970s-era white vinyl peel-and-stick floor with an intricate embossed pattern, creating numerous crevices for dirt to gather. After a couple of years of mere sweeping and spot cleaning, the floor had accumulated a noticeable layer of grime, its once-white color now best described as off-white. Armed with a sponge mop and bucket from the utility room, along with a container of Mop & Glo floor cleaner, I set to work.

With the table and chairs moved out, I stood at the corner near the refrigerator, sponge mop submerged in sudsy water. I assumed the task would be simple, but it didn't take long to realize the tiles wouldn't be easy to clean. The sponge mop's abrasive nylon edge was brought into play as I vigorously scrubbed each tile. An hour later, only half of the kitchen floor was tackled, my hands and arms fatigued and my motivation waning. To save the hassle of frequent bucket dips, I emptied the remaining cleaning solution and pushed the mop around the untouched half of the floor. The allure of a Saturday-morning cartoon beckoned from the television in the adjacent room, diverting my attention. About forty minutes later, I returned to the kitchen, mop in hand, and without much scrubbing, mopped up the cleaning solution puddles. An hour later, the floor was dry, and the table and chairs found their places once more.

Mimi returned from her errands, and as I helped with unloading groceries, I found myself on the receiving end of a reprimand for supposedly only cleaning half the floor. I defended my work, claiming to have mopped the entire floor. Mimi thought I was lying, and I felt frustrated and hurt. No matter what I said, I couldn't change her mind. As she headed toward the corner where I began hours earlier, she quipped, "This is dirty, and this is dirty. This entire half of the floor hasn't been mopped."

I put in a lot of effort, especially on the half Mimi said I hadn't cleaned. Although I cleaned the entire floor, comparing the halves didn't show it. It took me a while to understand what had happened. The cleaning solution I carelessly poured on the second half had more than thirty minutes to work, loosening and dissolving the dirt. With so little effort, that half became much cleaner, almost like new. It was disheartening to realize that most of the hard work I had put into the first part of the floor had gone to waste.

The task of mopping the kitchen floor became my twice-a-year responsibility. I had learned the simple and efficient technique of pouring and spreading the cleaning solution, waiting thirty minutes, and then mopping it up. It looked great but little did I know that I was creating unforeseen problems.

Dumping a bucket of water on the tiles caused issues: it got into the wood baseboards, dripped into the floor vents, and soaked the shag carpet in the adjacent rooms. Years later, in college, I realized the consequences of my cleaning shortcut. My mother mentioned the need to replace the kitchen flooring because the tiles were loose. It dawned on me that my soak-and-sit floor cleaning method may have been the cause of the adhesive's failure. I never told her what I had done or my suspicions.

The memory of my soak-and-sit floor cleaning still affects me and shapes my work ethic. The juxtaposition of the clean and dirty halves, mistakenly associated with hard work and laziness. But it wasn't until I was a professional that I questioned the overemphasis often placed on hard work. In my career's early stages, working hard was my only approach, but repeated failures brought back my floor-cleaning lesson: hard work doesn't always produce a clean floor—or bring success. Our best lessons often result from mistakes, forcing us to find smarter solutions. Over time, I understood the significance of working smarter and came to appreciate the beauty of simple solutions that reduced my effort while achieving the same results.

Teenage Independence and the Perception of Control

In the fall of 1978, I started my freshman year of high school wearing the only pair of bell-bottom jeans I ever owned, drinking beer, and jamming to 104.7 WTUE, Dayton's classic rock station. At fourteen, I had my independence and newfound freedom, invincibility, and control. I'd sneak out through my bedroom window to join friends around town or choose to ignore everyone and spend hours listening to music alone in my room.

Turntables were expensive, vinyl LPs were prone to scratches, and cassettes were gaining ground. That Christmas, Santa gifted me a portable cassette player, and I bought my first cassette tape,

Van Halen, at the local Ben Franklin. With Van Halen blasting on the radio, classic and southern rock left an indelible mark, nurturing a passion for bands I could only dream of seeing live: Lynyrd Skynyrd, The Outlaws, Molly Hatchet, and more. Their defiance of convention was inspiring during a period when I struggled to assert control over my own life.

Freshman year introduced the idea of college. Guidance counselors polled how many were planning to attend and a third of us raised our hands. I don't know what prompted me to raise my hand, but I knew I wanted to experience life beyond my childhood home.

The year 1978 also ushered in easy access to alcohol and marijuana, which seemed like exciting choices. I also felt a sense of control regarding my effort in high school sports, sometimes practicing and at other times taking a laid-back approach, a decision I would later regret.

THE EXTENT OF MY sex education with my mother occurred during my sixteenth birthday party. One of my gifts was a 45 RPM record by The Knack with a track entitled Good Girls Don't. My mother made a flippant comment: "You ever use that thing and I'll cut it off." I regret the lack of more thorough discussions about the risks of unprotected intercourse. Despite some sex education at school, a weekend on my own during my sophomore year and a movie date followed by drinking strongly influenced the night I became sexually active. While it didn't lead to life-altering consequences, it could have, and the thought of becoming a young parent through unprotected sex would have disrupted my plans for education. Pursuing a career as an Industrial Engineer or a job in California would have been distant dreams. Although I'm not discounting the potential for happiness in that scenario, it's hard to imagine it surpassing the fulfillment I've found and the love in my life today. The journey underscores how external influences and personal choices can significantly shape our paths.

GROWING UP, MOST OF my culinary experiences came from my mother's home-cooked meals. Because we frequently had dishes like hot dogs, goulash, and meatloaf, my fondness for these simple but comforting foods grew over time. Eating steak and dining out was rare due to our financial situation. It took years to recognize that these beloved dishes, the ones I craved, were actually some of the most affordable and convenient options. My love of Shake 'n Bake chicken wasn't about its taste; it was because I ate it twice a month during my teenage years. The control I felt during that time was just an illusion. My interests and my favorite foods were molded by my family's circumstances and our limited resources. We didn't have much, and my food preferences mirrored that reality.

As a young professional, I began dating women who were different from the girls I had known in high school or college. One remarkable woman I dated was a successful IBM salesperson, educated and accomplished. During a conversation about food, I mentioned my love for the Hardee's Mushroom and Swiss burger, a frequent snack during my first two years of college. I asked if she had ever tried Skyline Chili, a chain of Cincinnati-style chili eateries, which was also a personal favorite. Her response stunned me. Without judgment, she said, "I've never eaten fast food." I was taken aback, grappling with surprise and disbelief. She was clearly out of my league, but the encounter underscores how our experiences shape us and even influence the foods we like to eat.

Unexpected Leadership

In 1979, during my sophomore year of high school, an unexpected turn led me to become Vice President of the Student Council. This position resulted not from popularity or campaign efforts but from my friendship with a popular upperclassman who needed a running mate. This opportunity thrust me into an unexpected leadership role.

As members of the Student Council, we represented students to the School Board and the broader community. Our responsibilities included leading student assemblies and organizing events, with the fall homecoming parade being a standout task. This encompassed scheduling, route planning, participant coordination, and decorations.

My main responsibility involved coordinating car owners to transport the homecoming court, and male and female represent- atives from each class. Classic 1960s convertible Corvettes were the luxurious rides chosen for this role. The parade began at the high school and concluded within the football stadium, where cars cruised along the field's cinder track to drop off attendants.

One weekend during my sophomore year, when my family was away, also marked a turning point. Due to my mother's busy schedule and responsibilities with my younger siblings, my sister and I had minimal parental supervision and no fixed curfew. This lack of guidance led to mischief, particularly with my sister's older friends who were more experienced with alcohol, smoking, and other activities.

Shifting Gears – Fall 1980

Although I had been driving my sister's 1974 AMC Hornet for a year, my Huffy Scout 27-inch 10-speed bicycle remained my go-to escape vehicle from long summer days at home. However, this year, I rode it for a different reason. I was shifting away from team sports and embracing running and cycling. While team sports focus on working together and achieving goals as a group, doing individual activities let me set my own pace and goals, fostering a sense of personal accomplishment and independence. This marked the beginning of my lifelong passion for cycling. Interestingly, this was also the year when my mother grew less fond of the light blue sculpted pile carpet in the front room and dining room. Replacing the carpet was costly and not an option since it was still in good condition. One of her friends suggested the idea of dyeing the carpet ourselves. Intrigued by the prospect of such an easy and significant change, I ran with the idea.

I headed to our local Ben Franklin store and purchased cocoa brown RIT dye, a popular brand used for coloring textiles. Armed with a bucket of hot water, dye solution, and a carpet brush, I started the process. After days of soaking and brushing, the light blue carpet transformed into a deep shade of brown. However, I had thoroughly soaked the carpet, requiring three fans and four humid weeks to fully dry.

Surprisingly, it took over two years for the dye to fully set in the carpet. Walking on the carpet without shoes led to brown dye staining socks or bare feet. I'm amazed at my mother's trust in allowing me to dye the carpet. If my father had been alive, I might not have had this "opportunity." Growing up without him gave me a certain amount of freedom, as well as a duty, to explore both positive and negative opportunities at a younger age than my peers. My mother's belief and confidence in me as a young man have stayed with me throughout my life.

That same year, the idea of going to college started to take shape. Nobody in my extended family had ever been to college, but it just felt like the right path for me. I was pretty good at math, and I'd heard that the engineering college at the University of Cincinnati (UC) had a great reputation, especially for electrical engineering. Then, in my senior year of high school, my chemistry teacher mentioned that Tom Crawford, who was the valedictorian of the BHS class of 1981, was at UC's engineering program and struggling with college-level calculus. She was worried that I might have similar difficulties if I went to UC and suggested I think about going to Tri State College in Indiana instead. But that just made me more determined to go to UC's engineering program, even though it was known to be tougher than Tri State College. I also knew that UC had pioneered the world's first cooperative education program in engineering back in 1906. This history, along with UC's continued excellence in engineering, made me sure that UC was the right place for my higher education.

Fall 1981 – Small Town Denouement

In my senior year of high school, the urge to break free from home grew stronger every day. I remember this one time during a break in my English class when my friend Mark Polston and I were looking out of a second-floor window. Looking down at the school parking lot, I realized I knew the owners of all the cars—teachers, staff, and fellow students. Most of the cars were old and showed signs of wear and rust from the tough Ohio winters. Adjacent to the school, rows of simple houses lined the street, and I knew the residents of each one. It was a beautiful sunny day, and seeing everyone seemingly content made me turn to Mark and say, "We've got to get out of here." Despite being happy, we both knew that our potential for growth was limited in that small town; we needed to explore the wider world beyond Brookville.

My interests were shifting, with my disinterest in team sports continuing. I only participated in basketball that year, but my passion for it was fading and I focused on cycling instead. While I attended scheduled basketball practices, I skipped the extra workouts on Saturdays and during holidays. The impact of my lackadaisical approach became evident at the basketball banquet my senior year, where Coach Akers humorously commented, "... and Holsinger, he never made it to a single Saturday practice." His remark humiliated me and made me question whether I had forgotten everything I learned during those long summer days in the Dull corn fields.

Although I was committed to attending UC after graduation, I procrastinated applying for admission to the College of Electrical Engineering (EE). In January, a disappointing response that the EE program was full led me to my only option, Industrial Engineering (IE). It was a reaction rather than a deliberate choice. By the year's end, armed with an acceptance letter, I headed to UC to study industrial engineering.

1982 – College Bound

In the fall of 1982, I started my college journey at UC in the five-year engineering cooperative education work/study program. This unique program featured a structure where students attended classes in their first and fifth years while alternating between school and professional employment during the three middle years. During college orientation, a counselor shared a startling statistic, stating, "Look to your left and then to your right, only one of you in this program will graduate." Despite the unsettling remark, I brushed it off, thinking, "It can't be that hard."

During high school, I didn't have to study very much and graduated with honors, which had its disadvantages. It meant I hadn't developed effective study habits. As a result, by the end of my first quarter in college, I was barely scraping by in my physics and calculus courses and my chemistry teacher's words came back to haunt me. To avoid failing these classes, I isolated myself during the week, spending most hours not in class studying in the library. This demanding routine was something I hated. Every moment of my day was filled with attending class, eating, or studying. The only relief came when I could finally lay my head on a pillow and rest. I managed to make it through the year with a C+ average across all my classes, and I was glad to still be in school.

Moving into my second year, I became eligible to begin co-op work in January 1984. The competition for co-op positions was fierce, as there were more students than available jobs. Most first-year college students in 1983 had resumes with limited content, mainly comprising high school summer jobs and brief college activities. My own resume highlighted my high school involvements, such as being the Student Council President, participating in sports, and my work experiences, including roles as a residential vinyl siding installer, general contractor assistant, and farm crew leader. Outside the college career counselors' offices, a corkboard displayed job opportunities, and I applied for every co-op industrial engineering position listed, despite my unimpressive grades. Three companies reviewed my resume and offered me interviews. Among them, Huffy Bicycles in Celina, Ohio, extended an offer after an interview with Deral Rackley, Huffy's Industrial Engineering Manager.

1984 – Co-op Enlightenment

During my first work quarter in Huffy's Industrial Engineering Department, we acquired an IBM Personal Computer XT for running simulation software for time and motion studies. Due to my keen interest in new technology, I was chosen to operate the computer. As I set up the computer—a novel and sophisticated technology at the time—the entire department gathered around, intrigued by this cutting-edge addition to our workspace. I booted up the IBM PC-DOS from 5.25-inch floppy disks, formatted the 20MB hard drive, and installed the operating system along with Lotus 1-2-3 (the 1983 precursor to Microsoft Excel). That night, I took home all the operating manuals and studied them thoroughly, becoming the resident PC and Lotus 1-2-3 expert in Huffy's Industrial Engineering department.

At the end of my Huffy Bicycle co-op experience in the fall of 1985, I took on a part-time job alongside my college coursework, creating Lotus 1-2-3 spreadsheets for FIHC, a financial investment firm, using IBM's latest PC, the PC AT. The financial models involved hundreds of rows and columns, pushing the PC AT's memory limits. My responsibilities expanded to include being the technical lead for the firm's acquisition of the IBM System/36 midrange computer system. This role brought me into contact with a significant group of IBM professionals who would later influence my career and life.

As I entered my senior year, my co-op experience at Huffy Bicycles and my part-time jobs led me to realize that engineering wasn't my passion, which was stressful to me. I had invested five years in engineering studies only to discover that I didn't actually want to be an industrial engineer

My senior year of college in 1986, Ann Xanders, the manager

of IBM's sales team that supported the FIHC account, offered me a part-time role as a Marketing Sales Associate (MSA) at IBM and I supported the IBM sales team every week between my classes, handling IBM PS/2 PC installations and setups across the UC campus. On one day, I'd be tossing a hacky sack on the quad, on another, leading PS/2 orientation sessions, and on yet another, installing a PC in the Dean of Engineering assistant's office. I put in more hours working in my senior year than studying. My college journey, which had begun with challenges, appeared to be concluding on a positive and successful note.

The American Dream was coming into view, even if becoming an engineer wasn't going to be the route I took to achieve it. Later in life, I realized there wasn't a single path or choice I could have made that would guarantee my happiness.

UNHAPPY SUCCESS

"No one should ever ask themselves that: why am I unhappy? . . . If we ask that question, it means we want to find out what makes us happy. If what makes us happy is different from what we have now, then we must either change once and for all or stay as we are."
— Paulo Coelho, The Zahir

The Paradox of Winning

In a world obsessed with achievement—financial success, social recognition, professional awards—we often fail to question what "success" really means. By societal measures, I was doing well. A rewarding job, a stable life, and a decent social circle were all badges of a life well-lived, or so it seemed. But why did happiness elude me like a wisp of a cloud, always visible but never within reach?

I had everything I was told I should want, yet something within me remained unsatisfied, restless, and, paradoxically, unfulfilled. I felt like a marathon runner who had just crossed the finish line but didn't feel the exhilaration, the glory, or the satisfaction that should come with such an accomplishment. Instead, all I felt was an inexplicable emptiness, as if the race I had just run was on a loop, and I was back at the starting line.

In a deterministic universe, it felt like even my feelings of emptiness were predestined. Did this mean my pursuit of success, which in the end felt hollow, was something I couldn't avoid? It seemed like a cruel irony from the idea that we're all driven by self-interest. Society saw me as successful, yet these standards didn't match my deeper quest for fulfillment. If chasing happiness is naturally selfish, how did I end up so far off track? This questioning showed a clear difference between what society sees as success and the complex path to true happiness.

Understanding this discord requires retracing steps and questioning some very fundamental assumptions—not just about success and happiness, but also about the influence of determinism on them. It means dissecting the layers of cause and effect that had led me here, to a point where success felt less like an accomplishment and more like a complex riddle.

This is a dive into the murky waters of success and happiness—a narrative that draws from both the deterministic elements that shaped me and the selfish goals that propelled me forward. It's about unraveling why what should have been my happiest moments turned into a deep personal struggle, and understanding how to find my way through it.

Success and happiness are not always allies; in fact, they can be at odds. And sometimes, realizing that is the first step toward finding a more authentic version of yourself—a self that is both successful and happy.

Navigating Life's Course

Wolf Creek springs to life near Brookville, trickling its way through town. As a child, I'd leap from rock to rock across its shallow waters, occasionally looking for tadpoles or skipping stones along its surface. From its modest beginnings near Pleasant Plain Road, the creek eventually merges with the Miami River in Dayton. This larger river then joins the Ohio River, flowing further into the vast Mississippi and ultimately emptying into the Gulf of Mexico.

Water, propelled by gravity, possesses inherent potential energy that guides it along the path of least resistance. It flows naturally, seeking the most efficient route. However, its movement isn't unrestricted; it encounters obstacles—such as rocks, trees, and man-made barriers—that shape and limit its course. Once in motion, this water becomes a kinetic force, exerting influence on its environment through processes like erosion. In contrast, the still waters of a pond, despite their latent potential, remain stationary due to constraints and a lack of opportunity for movement.

This interplay of forces brings to mind the Grand Canyon, carved over nearly six million years by the persistent erosive power of the Colorado River. Over eons, the river navigated through layers of volcanic rock and sediment, following the only course available to it. Now, altering its path would require an immensely powerful intervention.

Our lives are shaped much like a river that gradually carves its course over many years through and around barriers and influences. Just as altering the course of the Colorado River would need a monumental effort, similarly, significant events or profound insights are typically required to change the trajectory of our lives.

The IBM Milestone: A Path Paved by Life

Could I have ever foreseen how my early days working in a cornfield with Ralph Dull at thirteen would chart the course of my professional journey? This early work experience set me apart in my co-op interview, which led me to IBM, giving me a crucial foothold in the tech world through my work on IBM PCs and Lotus 1-2-3. This chapter in my life would eventually see me sitting across from Mark Doran, the Branch Manager of IBM's Cincinnati office, my heart pounding as I prepared for what I thought would be a grueling interview—only to hear him say, "You've got the job. What questions can I answer for you?"

Despite my technical engineering background, I found myself offered a sales role at IBM. It was a door that opened for me with little effort and I was too inexperienced to recognize or contemplate that I might have other options. Of course, I took the offer without hesitation or thought that there might be alternatives. I recognized IBM's world-class reputation. It felt like I was on the upswing: about to graduate from college, job offer in hand, and seemingly set for the future.

During finals week, I found myself wrestling with a particularly challenging course. I pulled an all-nighter, relying on NoDoz—a caffeine pill—to stay alert. I'd experimented with various means to stay awake during college, but by this point, I was focused and had sworn off stimulants. I aced the exam the next day and managed to fit in a drug test for IBM that afternoon.

A week later, a call from IBM HR shook me: my urine sample was misplaced, and I needed to retake the test. This time, the clinic had a more thorough process requiring my signature on the bottle and the box it was sealed in, perhaps to avoid another blunder. After a hearty night of celebration, I managed to make it through my college graduation and reported for my first day at IBM the next week.

While settling into my new role, I met Mark Lacefield, a teammate who ribbed me about failing my first drug test. Panic washed over me as I pondered the situation and ramifications. Despite my dread, it was a non-issue—I had disclosed taking NoDoz, an over-the-counter drug. I can only assume it was the reason I failed that first test. It seemed I had barely dodged a bullet and only because someone was willing to give me a second chance.

Within three months, I was enrolled in IBM's Sales School, a year-long intensive program that taught us everything from managing customer accounts to selling IBM products. There, I met a bunch of new colleagues, including a cute female trainee from Detroit who quickly became a close friend. Even though we were hundreds of miles apart, we began instant messaging across the country on IBM 3270 green screen terminals. It felt like magic.

IBM Cincinnati's social environment also provided opportunities for connection and career development. One evening at happy hour, Mark Doran joined us. He engaged in light conversation about our clients like General Electric and Procter &

Gamble, as well as local sports teams like the Cincinnati Reds and Cincinnati Bengals. At one point he directly engaged me and asked, "What do you want to do at IBM?" I found myself stumped. All I could articulate were the things I didn't want to do. "I don't want to be a Systems Engineer, work in the Customer Center, or be in marketing." And before I could take a breath, Mark cut me off and said, **"Don't tell me what you *don't* want to do, tell me what you *want* to do."**

Up until this point, my life had been more about avoiding things that were painful rather than pursuing something that would bring me joy other than a degree and a job. Discussions about happiness, life's deeper meanings, or even our motivations were absent from my family narrative. We lived day-to-day, rooted in practicalities, never questioning the deeper 'why' behind our choices.

In that moment, as I stood there speechless in front of my branch manager, it hit me that I didn't know what I wanted.

There was no way to express my wants and desires that did not exist beyond *that* job at IBM. The significance of Mark's question would only become clear over the course of many years. Not only did I not know what I wanted to do, I realized I didn't even know how to begin to figure it out. Eventually, I came to a painful realization: the life I was living wasn't driven by the pursuit of happiness, but rather the avoidance of potentially painful situations.

This chapter in my life was an early indication of how my path was not entirely my own, but rather shaped by a myriad of external influences. While I felt like I was making choices, my choices were driven by practical needs and obviously all that was presented to me. Much like water flowing down a predetermined path. At that moment, happiness seemed elusive to me because it wasn't a primary consideration in my decision-making process. It was something I hadn't consciously thought about or discussed with another person.

Connections Matter

The bonds we forge are pivotal in shaping our lives, giving us both emotional grounding and purpose. Family—our first and often deepest connection—provides a unique layer of support, derived from shared history, heritage, and unconditional love. Whether you're born into a family or become part of one through marriage and children, the ties can be equally strong. For example, my parents were joined by matrimony, not genetics, and yet they built a family together. After my father passed away, my mother remarried, and my stepfather became as much a part of my family as any blood relative. Later in life, I took on the role of stepparent, loving my stepdaughter as if she were my own.

Beyond family, friendships and romantic partnerships add nuanced layers to our web of relationships. Friendships are voluntary but essential unions, grounded in mutual interests and experiences. Marriages, on the other hand, are a mosaic of emotional, romantic, and practical considerations where life is built in shared responsibility and mutual growth.

It took me years, a divorce, and a near-death experience to fully grasp the importance of these connections. After I left home, I realized I'd already spent the bulk of the time I would ever spend with my family. Life circumstances, including my father's passing, had a domino effect, setting me on a path from farming with Dull Homestead to a corporate role at IBM. It was during a low moment, lying in a hospital bed in 2016, that I began to ponder the interwoven threads that had shaped my life's journey.

My passion for cycling re-ignited during my college days when I worked at Huffy Bicycles. It all began after I rode twenty-five miles during the Huffy Celina manufacturing plant's summer 1985 employee picnic. While working at IBM, I trained with colleagues and completed the much more demanding 112-mile Solvang Century bicycle ride in northern California. This enthusiasm in long distance events evolved over time, eventually leading me to partic-ipate in endurance sports like marathons. However, a foot injury during marathon training in 2005 redirected me toward cycling and swimming, ultimately immersing me in the triathlon community.

Success, when achieved through hard work, brings its own kind of exhilaration. The training and endurance needed to complete a 100-mile ride are born out of sheer determination and tenacity. But as I focused intently on sports, training for increasingly challenging events like the Half Ironman Triathlon, my life outside of athletics began to unravel.

During this period, I met Barry Conlon at a 24 Hour Fitness indoor cycling class, who later introduced me to the Bat City Cycling Club (BCCC). Little did I know then that this introduction would be a critical piece in the mosaic of circumstances that led to a life-altering accident. Before reaching that point, however, I found myself in a spiral of obsessive training, a means of avoiding the reality that my marriage was falling apart.

The complex web of relationships and experiences in my life serves as an enlightening example. Relationships are not just social constructs; they are lifelines that shape us, sustain us, and sometimes lead us down paths we'd never have anticipated. Whether we like it or not, they form the narrative of our lives, requiring us to continuously evaluate and understand the roles we play in the grand scheme of things.

The Influence of Individual Experiences

My uniqueness in a world of over eight billion people stems from a complex blend of my genetic makeup ("nature") and my life experiences ("nurture"). While genes provide the blueprint, determining aspects like my eye color or natural inclinations, it's the interaction with my environment that truly defines me.

Influence is a multifaceted concept. It's the power to affect someone's decisions or actions and comes from many sources—our families, communities, or even public figures. Take a family of musicians influencing a child toward a musical career; it may seem like a personal choice, but it's heavily influenced by the environment in which they grew up.

Influence isn't just from the outside; it's also about how we respond to our inner needs. If you opt for a fitness routine after reading about its health advantages, it might appear as if you were influenced by expert advice. Another perspective suggests you're simply fulfilling your self-interest to attain a healthier, longer life.

HUMAN DEVELOPMENT, A MULTIDISCIPLINARY field within psychology, explores how individuals grow and change over their lives. This field encompasses everything from how our personalities form to how we gather knowledge and wealth. Some key figures in this area include the following:

Erik Erikson was an ego psychologist who examined the impact of social experiences throughout an individual's life. He theorized that personality develops in a predetermined order through eight stages of **psychosocial development**, from infancy to adulthood. During each stage, the person experiences a psychosocial crisis which could have a positive or negative outcome for personality development.

Jean Piaget developed the theory of **cognitive development**, realizing that child brains had different abilities than adult brains. In his theory, mental processes were reorganized in four age-related stages based on experiences: *Sensorimotor* (birth to two years), *Preoperational* (ages two to seven), *Concrete Operational* (ages seven to eleven), *Formal Operational* (ages twelve and up). He concluded that children were not less intelligent than adults, they simply think differently. Intelligence grows and develops as we age.

Lawrence Kohlberg's theory is based on **moral development**. His theory has three stages: *Preconventional* (where people follow rules because they're afraid of punishment), *Conventional* (where people act to avoid society's judgment and follow rules), and *Postconventional* (where people have a genuine concern for the welfare of others and the greater good of society).

Sigmund Freud is famous for the **psychosexual theory** which focuses on a person's development between birth and adolescence. This theory emphasizes how individuals navigate and resolve conflicts related to their basic instincts and social interactions, influencing their personality and behavior in adulthood. Freud's work laid the foundation for understanding the intricate interplay between biology and early life experiences in shaping human development.

Other theories, like **Behavioral Theory** and **Social Learning Theory** stress the role of behavior and social observation, respectively, in personal development. **Sociocultural theory**, on the other hand, emphasizes the role society and culture play in shaping an individual.

The common thread among these theories is the **crucial role of personal experiences** in defining who we are. The person I am today has been molded by a series of life events, many of which were beyond my control. My ethics were shaped by influences from my parents, peers, family, and religious upbringing. Childhood experiences, like being bullied, made me cautious in social situations. My time as a Boy Scout and stepping up as the man of the house after my father's passing instilled in me a strong sense of self-reliance and responsibility. The tight-knit community of my hometown left a lasting imprint, as did life lessons from experiences such as moving to Cincinnati for college only to have my belongings stolen upon arrival or feeling deceived during my first home purchase.

In essence, the path of my life, marked by these significant experiences, has not only influenced who I am but also shaped my view of the world in ways both subtle and profound.

The Elusive Quest for Happiness

Finding genuine happiness has been challenging for me. When you're not even sure what ignites your inner joy, how do you go about attaining happiness? While my family and friends contributed moments of happiness, the complexities of adulthood introduced a host of new challenges.

Our early perceptions of happiness are molded by our families and communities. Yet, as we mature, we increasingly shoulder the burden of making our own choices, often exploring various activities for temporary satisfaction. The promise of the American Dream—that dedication and hard work would lead to prosperity and happiness—motivated me to leave my hometown in pursuit of higher education.

Early in my career with IBM, I relocated to California, chasing my dreams. I became engaged, purchased a house, and went to work each day. But contentment eluded me. Before I turned thirty, I had been through two broken engagements. I eventually married a girl from my hometown, but my soul always yearned for something indefinable. I had assumed that shared values and common past experiences with her would create lasting happiness, but despite appearances, and even having children, I remained unfulfilled.

On the surface, everything seemed fine. I was managing my daily responsibilities and even finding moments of joy in family life. However, my career in tech sales was a different story. It felt like a relentless, soul-sucking routine. Despite the facade of normalcy, I secretly loathed my job, which consisted of the same tedious tasks, just at different companies over the years. Each week, the highlight was the arrival of Friday at 5:00 PM, when I'd indulge in a cocktail mix of Seagram's 7 Crown whiskey and 7-Up. I convinced myself that this ritual was a well-deserved reward, but in truth, it was a coping mechanism—a sign of deeper, unresolved issues with the path my life had taken.

After welcoming our third child into the world, I found myself grappling with mounting frustrations rather than experiencing pure unhappiness. My former wife and I were swamped, juggling our demanding careers while attending to our children's educational and extracurricular needs.

In 2009, one particularly chaotic weekend served as a prime example: our kids, aged thirteen, nine, and four, had a jam-packed itinerary involving two birthday parties and six soccer games. My former wife and I adopted a divide-and-conquer strategy, each of us shuttling the kids to their various commitments throughout central Texas. While we found some satisfaction in managing to keep the schedule, the frenzy left no room for attending to the health of our relationship.

Such diversions, like coordinating an action-packed weekend, often acted as smoke screens for underlying unhappiness. Retrospectively, it's evident that I spent a considerable part of my married life in a state of discontent. This emotional fog made it difficult to identify the unhappiness that had subtly woven itself into the fabric of my life.

One telling moment occurred during dinner preparations. When my former wife asked for my preference, my reply was indifferent: "I don't know, it doesn't matter." Unbeknownst to me, my indifference sent her a clear message—that I didn't care about her, our family, or even our relationship. My disengagement was obvious, leading to escalating tensions and disputes.

I believed I was earnest in my efforts to make my former wife happy, but I eventually realized that we had unconsciously adopted a "children-first" strategy to our family dynamic. While well-intentioned, this approach often meant that our own needs took a backseat. And so, in an attempt to manufacture joy, I invested heavily in experiences and material possessions—from lavish Disney Cruise and Dixie Dude Ranch vacations to the latest video games and gadgets, no expense was spared in my attempt to buy us happiness.

However, my well-laid plans hit a snag when my former wife confronted me one afternoon about feeling left out of our vacation planning. Frustrated, I retorted, "Why don't you plan the next one? In fact, no more vacations unless you take charge." That moment felt like a tipping point; it was as if I had thrown in the towel on our marriage. Exhausted, I was awash in conflicting emotions, painfully aware of my inability to bring her happiness; this obliterated any responsibility I felt for her joy.

This period of introspection led me to an uncomfortable truth: I could never make someone else happy, just as they couldn't make me happy. At that point, I resolved to focus on my own well-being, even though I lacked a clear roadmap. While I couldn't ignore my responsibilities as a parent, I found myself merely going through the motions. I had emotionally disengaged, and the harmonious family life we once imagined became an elusive dream.

Cause-and-Effect Relationships

Determinism is the philosophical belief that all events are pre-determined by prior events. It posits that given a specific set of conditions, only one outcome is possible. However, determinism as a general concept does not necessarily make a claim about the existence or non-existence of free will.

Various forms of determinism have been postulated to explain the complexities of human experience and behavior. **Hard Determinism** is a more specific form of determinism that not only asserts that the future is already determined but also **denies the existence of free will**. According to hard determinism, humans are not morally responsible for their actions because they have no control over them; their actions were determined by an unbroken chain of prior events. **Causal determinism** deals exclusively with the principle of cause and effect. It posits that every event is necessitated by antecedent events and conditions together with the laws of nature. In other words, it's the belief that any state (or event) is determined by prior states (or events) in a manner described by natural laws.

Soft determinism, or compatibilism, proposes that free will can coexist with determinism, albeit with different interpretations of what "free will" means. Under this viewpoint, individuals can still bear moral responsibility for their actions.

Predeterminism shares similarities with theological predestination and posits that all events are determined by a higher power, such as a deity.

The question of whether humans have free will is a deeply unsettling one for many people. I personally faced this challenging issue after going through a catastrophic accident.

While some forms of determinism liken humans to billiard balls, with our actions being mere reactions to the environment, this is not universally accepted across all deterministic philosophies. In this view, each interaction we have subtly changes us, much like constant collisions between billiard balls. Yet, it's essential to note that other perspectives, such as soft determinism, allow for a greater degree of free will and moral responsibility, even within a deterministic framework. The question of life's purpose often becomes complex and challenging when considering these varying stances on determinism.

The principle of causality holds that every event has a precursor that caused it. The Big Bang is commonly seen as the initial event that gave rise to our universe as we understand it in space-time. However, it's important to clarify that the causative factors behind the Big Bang itself remain a subject of ongoing research and philosophical debate. For humans, who are constrained by our perception of a three-dimensional spatial world coupled with time, the Big Bang represents the earliest event we can presently comprehend as having a causative role in the universe's history.

If we pay attention in life, we will notice recurring patterns. A cause-and-effect dynamic is constantly happening around us. For instance, during my college years, if I dedicated a couple of nights to studying for an exam (cause), I would achieve a good grade (effect). On the other hand, if I got sidetracked by socializing with my college roommates and went out for dinner and drinks instead (cause), my academic performance would suffer (effect). Similarly, in my professional life, failing to make a hundred sales calls every week (cause) would result in falling short of my quarterly sales quota (effect). And again, to maintain my fitness, I started running (cause), which led to weight loss (effect).

It should hardly come as a shock that events are connected, and recognizing patterns or cause-and-effect relationships can give us the sense of having some control over what comes next. This illusion was shattered for me one day during a long run. Just as I was growing tired, I stepped off a curb and twisted my ankle. In that instant, the idea of control came into question. How could I have control in choosing to go for a run, but lack control over something as random as twisting my ankle? That moment was a reminder that the concept of control is more complex than we assume.

The Chaos of Control: A Heroic Yet Flawed Rescue

The Club is a bright red anti-theft device for automobiles that was invented in the 1980s. It is designed to be inserted, extended, and locked through the steering wheel. While it serves as a visual deterrent, it does not eliminate the possibility of a break-in and theft. However, it effectively immobilizes the steering wheel, making it difficult for thieves to steer the vehicle. One morning during my commute to my sales job at TEKsystems, I encountered a chaotic scene of an active automobile accident. I was travelling on a divided two-lane highway. In the turning lane to my left, there were cars, bumper-to-bumper, stopped at a traffic signal. I saw a silver Nissan Sentra that I presumed had forcefully accelerated and slammed into the car stopped directly in front of it. The Sentra's front bumper was wedged under the rear bumper of the car ahead, its engine roaring and tires spinning, squealing, and emitting smoke from the burning tire tread. Without hesitation, I pulled my vehicle off the highway, jumped out of my Chevy Tahoe, and sprinted to the scene of the accident. Being the first person to arrive, I met the driver from the car in front just as she was approaching the Sentra. At the Sentra driver's door, I encountered a young male experiencing full body convulsions and foaming at the mouth.

My thinking became somewhat irrational at this sight. The Sentra's spinning tires and smoke coming from under the car added to the urgency. I felt that I had to get the young man out of the Sentra. The car, with spinning tires, could break free at any moment, potentially killing him or others nearby. As I tugged on the door handle, I realized it was locked, refusing to budge. Breaking the window seemed like the only option, but the median was all grass, no rocks or any other suitable objects. In a moment of quick thinking, I rushed back to my Tahoe and grabbed the only piece of metal I could find—The Club. I hurried back to the Sentra.

I swung The Club at the driver's door, shattering the glass. However, my subsequent actions didn't make sense. I reached inside the window frame and pulled with all my strength. But the door, locked and closed, remained stationary, causing shards of glass to cut my left palm, resulting in a bleeding cut. Unaware of my injury, I continued to try to open the door. If I had been in control of myself and the situation, I would not have grabbed a locked door and injured my hand. Clear thinking and control of my emotions would have led me to reach through the broken window and turn off the ignition, thereby stopping the engine's roar and the spinning tires. Perhaps I would have recognized the driver's seizure much sooner—his rigid leg and foot pressing the gas pedal to the floor. Regrettably, none of these realizations occurred to me. Overwhelmed by the circumstances, I was unable to make rational decisions; I could not exercise appropriate control.

Amidst the chaos, it finally dawned on me that I could unlock and open the car door. Once the door was open, my focus was to get the man out of the vehicle. I grabbed him by the chest, but to my dismay, he remained immobile. It was then that I had another moment of realization: he was still wearing his seatbelt. It made me question the purpose of our complex brains if we fail to notice the most obvious details when they matter the most.

Unbuckling the seatbelt, I was able to pull him out of the car. Despite feeling shaken, I managed to move him to a safe distance as his seizures persisted. A small group of individuals had gathered at the scene of the accident. One person with medical training began assisting the injured driver while another individual reached into the car and shut off the engine.

The police and EMS arrived at the scene and started assisting the driver. A medic noticed the blood on my hand and shirt and approached me, offering help. I explained that I wasn't involved in the accident but had injured myself while rescuing the driver. He seemed slightly surprised as he took my hand and began preparing it for my trip to the hospital emergency room. "You're a hero," he declared.

I contacted my office and provided an explanation for my absence from the morning's meetings. Once I received the necessary stitches and tended to my wounds at the ER, I managed to make it to work later that day. As I walked in and through the bullpen, the entire office staff of thirty people stood up, clapped, and congratulated me. It was at that moment that I truly grasped the significance of what had transpired that morning. I expressed my gratitude to everyone, turned away, and closed the door to my office, feeling a welling of post-stress tears in my eyes.

While I believed I had control over my actions when I decided to step out of my vehicle that morning, everything that unfolded afterward was a series of reactions to a chaotic situation. The circumstances were beyond my control, and my responses were purely instinctual rather than deliberate choices. At a primal level, I was reacting to the moment and my decisions were less than ideal. Looking back, those actions that seemed logical in the midst of the chaos, now appear puzzling and disjointed. Though I succeeded in saving the man's life, I can't help but feel a lingering sense of regret, wishing I had approached the situation with more composure, objectivity, and a comprehensive understanding of all potential outcomes. In essence, I wish I had been more in control of myself and the situation.

Group Influence

Imagine growing up in a small, rural community deeply rooted in farming traditions. If you find yourself drawn to a career in agriculture, is it truly a matter of personal choice, or is it an inevitable result of your upbringing? In a deterministic universe, the concept of 'influence' becomes more than just persuasive interactions; it's seen as a predestined element of your existence. Growing up surrounded by fields and tractors, the likelihood of becoming a farmer might seem less about active decision-making and more a foregone conclusion set by your environment.

Although we often believe we choose our friends, living locations, and professions, certain aspects like family lineage, gender, ethnicity, and place of birth are predetermined. These immutable factors, along with the communities we become part of—either by choice or circumstance—shape us in ways we may not fully realize. This led me to ponder how I became a member of specific groups and how these associations have influenced who I am today. A group is defined as two or more people interacting with each other, sharing norms and responsibilities, and having a mutual sense of belonging. In this sense, society itself could be considered a vast, complex group, although most of the groups we encounter in daily life are much smaller in scale.

Social dynamics refer to how a group influences its members' individual behaviors. Upon entering a group, you tacitly, if not explicitly, endorse its goals, ethics, and values. Your most significant influences are usually your family, friends, colleagues, or schoolmates. When a group's members share similar interests, a synergistic effect emerges, fostering camaraderie and a shared sense of purpose. This can be a positive form of influence, especially when the group is supportive and united in its objectives. However, on the flip side, group influence can turn negative if members cease to exhibit desired behaviors. Groups have built-in corrective measures that activate when someone strays from the accepted norms, sometimes leading to exclusion from the group. Thus, groups wield immense power in influencing our actions and choices.

In my hometown of 4,000 people everyone knew each other and along with formal laws at the city, state, and federal levels, there were also unwritten societal rules that governed our behavior. Many of these norms were etiquettes such as showing respect to elders and expressing basic manners like saying "please" and "thank you." While not everyone adhered to these norms, the consequences for breaking them were typically insignificant. However, other offenses had more significant consequences. Acts like infidelity or bullying, though not illegal, were deemed appalling by many. Over fences, neighbors and social groups discussed scandalous behavior and the people involved. These conversations were driven by boredom and curiosity rather than malice.

Gossip spread rapidly throughout the town, resulting in everyone knowing about each other's actions. This had consequences. It impacted social standing, reputation, and trust within the community. Gossip became a tool for manipulating and influencing those who caught the attention of others in town, making them feel shame and guilt.

To prevent expulsion, you conform to and exhibit the desired behavior dictated by the group. The process of expelling non-believers or non-conformists is built into the social dynamics of the group, serving an inherent process of group cleansing.

The citizenship of a country represents a unique social group that may not be immediately apparent. Unlike other social groups, individuals enter into a social contract with their country at birth, and there is an unspoken commitment to cooperate with one another for the collective welfare. The primary benefits of this social contract are safety and security, while the costs involve the payment of taxes and the loss of certain personal freedoms. This social contract works because, for the most part, we rely on each other for survival. We depend on farmers for food production, power companies for electricity, and the presence of police officers, firefighters, and military personnel for protection.

Regardless of their nature or size, all groups can have a significant influence on our behavior. The hormone oxytocin, which is known for its role in fostering social bonds, has been shown to facilitate affiliation toward an in-group. Sports, in particular, foster strong in-group dynamics. In these groups, qualities like competence, commitment, and consistent practice are highly valued. Hierarchies exist, such as first team and second team, starters and substitutes, and team captains. I recall my elementary school days when we played games like tag on the playground. The boys who were part of the Pee Wee football team formed a tight-knit group that was evident to everyone. They always stuck together and displayed superior athleticism compared to the rest of us. Initially, I couldn't fully grasp the dynamics of their group, and I yearned to be part of it. However, as I grew taller, leaner, stronger, and faster, I gradually found myself becoming a member of their group without even realizing it. I belonged because I exhibited the necessary qualities to be a valued member of the group.

During my early days as a professional at IBM, I experienced hazing from the seasoned IBM salesmen. While some of the hazing was done in good spirits, most of it was cruel and unpleasant. One incident occurred during a weekend meeting at a hotel. On the first night, while having a drink at the bar with my team members, someone asked whether I had a nice room, "Hey, where's your room? What's your room number?" Naively, I shared the details, only to discover upon checking out on Sunday morning that I had been pranked with a $200 bar charge from Friday night. It seemed this was a prank played on unsuspecting rookies. Unfortunately, I witnessed similar despicable behavior for years.

Although IBM took steps to address behavior like this through education and increased oversight, when I joined SAP years later, I was shocked to find that the behavior exhibited by their salesmen was worse than anything I had experienced at IBM. I never compromised my morals by participating in the hazing and learned to blend in with the sales teams to avoid becoming a target or an outcast, but it was never a comfortable environment for me.

CONFORMITY ACTS AS THE GLUE holding a group together. But what happens to group members who don't conform to the group's norms? Depending on the group's moral standards, these individuals may be ignored, chastised, or excluded. In extreme cases, a group might resort to harming or eliminating (killing) members who hold contrasting beliefs or exhibit variant behaviors. The group aims to maintain its purity by purging those who don't fit; it serves as a strong reminder that participation requires behavior acceptable to the group.

As a U.S. citizen, it's somewhat startling to realize that I belong to a group that supports the use of capital punishment for acts of treason against the country. The federal government actually lists over forty-one offenses that could lead to the death penalty. It's sobering to realize that such severe punishments are for non-conformity.

The Shifting Sands of Morality

In the U.S., slaughtering a cow is acceptable, but harming or consuming dog meat is not. Most Americans consider eating dog meat immoral—a sentiment that is largely influenced by dogs' historical role as companions in our country.

Morality varies across geographies, societies, and according to our personal experiences, and it shifts with society's evolution. My morals were influenced largely by religion and growing up in a very small town where everyone's morals were on display and gossip about one's morals had the power to shape conduct. Like all children, I faced moments of moral conflict, one of which occurred when I was eleven and succumbed to the temptation of stealing licorice taffy. Remarkably, the weight of this misdeed was effortlessly lifted off my shoulders with a simple confession to a priest, underscoring the stark disparity between the act and the ease of obtaining absolution. As a teenager, I drank alcohol and drove under its influence. At the time it was considered harmless fun. Today, it is considered extremely dangerous and deserving of severe punishment. Morals are also subjective and can become outdated. This challenges the notion of 'universal morality' and raises the question: Which of our current morals will future generations find illogical or barbaric?

Morality has always been a mix of influences, including religious beliefs, family values, social norms, and even observations of animals. In my own experience, the moral teachings of my childhood revolved around clear-cut issues like theft and killing. I learned that stealing was unacceptable, a lesson reinforced more by the fear of legal repercussions and parental punishment than by an innate sense of wrongness. Similarly, killing was framed as universally bad, even though my Uncle Philip's military service in Vietnam created a dissonance that led me to question the very foundation of such moral absolutes.

The notion of objective morality argues for the existence of fixed, immutable moral laws that hold true across diverse contexts and individual viewpoints. However, the actions and decisions of humans frequently challenge these so-called moral absolutes, casting a spotlight on the subjective and ever-changing nature of ethical values. Take, for example, the Victorian era, a period characterized by stringent social codes that emphasized virtues like chastity and discipline. These norms have since dissolved, replaced by advocacy for equality, workers' rights, and social justice as the 20th century unfolded.

The concept of altruism—selfless care for others—emerged during this time and became a central tenet of modern morality. With social and political movements bringing issues of shared responsibility and social equality into focus, altruism became synonymous with being a 'good' person. Yet, as history has shown, morality is never stagnant. Our society's evolving definitions of good and bad, or right and wrong, demonstrate the fluidity of moral beliefs. The struggle for civil rights and gender equality in the United States illustrates how what's considered virtuous can change dramatically within a few generations. Even our understanding of animal welfare has evolved, as public sentiment has moved against the captivity of killer whales like Tilikum, shifting moral ground once again.

In our current age, with its heightened focus on mental health and self-care, traditional virtues like altruism and selflessness are being critically reexamined. As we delve deeper into the human psyche, we're discovering that constantly prioritizing others over oneself may not always be virtuous, but rather a pathway to emotional burnout and psychological harm. This growing emphasis on self-care may well pave the way for a new moral framework, challenging long-standing virtues and inviting us to redefine what it means to lead a 'good' or 'virtuous' life.

The moral lessons of my upbringing, shaped as they were by fear and contradiction, serve as a testament to the fluid nature of ethical norms. As we look ahead, the rising importance of self-care and individual well-being could reshape our collective moral landscape, compelling us to rethink and revise what we consider to be virtues worth striving for.

The Las Vegas Epiphany: Challenging the Notion of Chance

As I grew up, traditional sayings like "actions speak louder than words" and "the grass is always greener" shaped my worldview. These adages, often recited by my parents and grandparents who had a modest formal education, influenced my early understanding of life. My family's knowledge was limited but foundational, stemming from community wisdom, limited media, and a few local newspapers like the *Dayton Daily News*. They believed in the simple notion that a stable job could ensure basic necessities like food and shelter.

As I went through a more comprehensive K-12 educational system, I began to realize that every generation perpetuates certain beliefs and knowledge, often regardless of its veracity. For instance, my father always assumed that a cloudy sky meant impending rain. His pronouncements led to many mornings of unnecessary raincoat-wearing on the way to school. In retrospect, it's clear that his understanding of statistical likelihoods was limited.

In our family, the coin toss was a popular method to settle minor disputes, from choosing a piece of candy to claiming the front seat of the car. As kids, my sister and I considered this a perfectly fair and random selection process. Only later did I discover that a coin toss is not entirely random.

Years later, while at a breakfast bistro in Las Vegas, I reminisced with college buddies about probability, especially as it applies to casino games like blackjack and roulette. During this conversation, I began to question the very concept of randomness. After an unfortunate stint at the blackjack table, I found myself trying to explain my string of losses by challenging the notion that a coin flip was a game of pure chance. I argued that if one were to account for multiple variables like the coin's design and flipping method, the outcome could theoretically be predicted. Though my friends were not entirely convinced, the idea remained lodged in my mind for years to come, resurfacing whenever I pondered life's uncertainties.

Today, I've come to understand that a coin toss isn't entirely random. Not only does it have a one in 6,000 chance of landing on its edge, but the face it starts on also has a slightly higher probability of landing face-up. The chances are not perfectly even; it's about fifty-one percent in favor of the starting face. Further complicating the odds are factors like the design of the coin, which in the United States usually has a heavier head design. If a coin is spun on its edge, there's an up to eighty percent chance it will land with the heavier side down, influencing the outcome even more.

Probability does not necessarily imply randomness. Everything from a tossed coin to life's bigger questions operates under laws and variables that could, in theory, be accounted for. The intricacies of probability have evolved in my understanding from simple childhood beliefs to a nuanced appreciation of the variables that shape outcomes.

The Paradox of Human Free Will: A Cosmic Anomaly

As I delved into research for my manuscript "No Time," I found myself compelled to study the origins of the universe, starting from the Big Bang. This exploratory journey opened my eyes to some remarkable facts. The universe began with a colossal burst of energy billions of years ago, setting the stage for a plethora of life forms. This chronology of life traces back to single-cell organisms that emerged approximately 1.9 billion years ago, evolved into dinosaurs around 240 million years ago, and culminated in the appearance of early modern humans about 49,000 years ago.

This knowledge led me to a startling philosophical quandary. The very biological material that catalyzed life on Earth had no capacity for free will or self-governance. Yet, there exists a widely accepted belief that this same elemental matter gained the faculties of free will and agency upon evolving into a human being.

The paradox is nothing short of mind-bending. How is it that the same raw materials, which began as basic single-cell life forms and were subjected to the forces of natural selection over eons, are now considered capable of free will exclusively when constituting a human? This raises the perplexing question of how free will could possibly arise spontaneously in one specific species, while the rest of the biological spectrum ostensibly operates without it.

To articulate this further, we face an intriguing cycle: humans come into existence without control, attain full control and free will during their lifetimes, only to have that control stripped away as they approach the inevitability of death.

This theory suggests an abrupt and extraordinary departure from a billion-year evolutionary trajectory, implying that free will is not just a rarity, but a unique privilege conferred solely upon human life on Earth. This view conflicts with both empirical evidence and the principles of evolutionary continuity, adding another layer of complexity to the already intricate debate over the nature of free will and agency in the universe.

Cognitive Shortcuts in Learning and Decision Making

I'll never forget that twilight evening when I first cycled without training wheels. With a gentle nudge from my father, I pedaled down the sidewalk, feeling as if I'd covered a vast distance before finally tipping over. In reality, I'd only made it four houses away. The emotional weight of that experience as a four-year-old has turned it into an enduring memory, especially poignant now that my father is no longer with me. Sometimes, the most emotionally charged moments, no matter how seemingly trivial, etch themselves permanently into our minds.

Memories form the building blocks of our learning process. We experience, we store, and we learn. It sounds straightforward, but our minds are complex systems with limitations. It's effortless to lose concentration and overlook important experiences that could be transformed from fleeting short-term memories into stable long-term ones. There are techniques to boost this transformation—like focused attention, repetition, and various forms of cognitive linking. These not only help in memory creation but also facilitate easier memory retrieval later on.

My recent encounter with a couple who share my niece's and nephew's names illustrates this. By connecting these new acquaintances with preexisting family memories, remembering their names became an almost automatic process. Such associative learning simplifies our cognitive tasks, making memory retention and retrieval more efficient.

Traditional classrooms can be unforgiving for those with learning disabilities, myself included. I only discovered the underlying cause of my struggles ten years post-college, but I had instinctively developed cognitive shortcuts to cope. My difficulty in shifting between visual and auditory learning modes meant that I had to spend extra time reviewing notes to commit them to long-term memory. Despite these obstacles, the necessity drove me to harness the brain's ability for heuristic solutions.

The brain's tendency to use shortcuts isn't a bug; it's a feature—one that's evolutionary in nature. These cognitive workarounds have been instrumental in human survival, helping us to swiftly recognize patterns, stereotype for quicker social navigation, and selectively attend to relevant stimuli in a sea of information. These shortcuts are our cognitive coping mechanisms for a world teeming with complexities.

Similarly, the practice of relying on recommendations from trusted sources—be it for finding a roofing contractor or casting a vote in an election—serves as another kind of cognitive shortcut. It helps in conserving mental resources but comes with the peril of oversimplification. It forces us into categorical boxes, overshadowing the nuanced understanding of complex issues, such as those in politics.

We are creatures of habit. Repetition not only aids in learning but also provides a comforting sense of familiarity. This repetitiveness, born from our survival instincts, often makes us resistant to change, whether it's in our taste preferences or even our emotional attachments, like the lifelong bond with our parents.

So, while cognitive shortcuts and repetition help us navigate the convoluted corridors of life, it's crucial to be discerning. Reflect on the repetitive elements and influences in your life. Keep what enriches you, and discard what diminishes you. Remember, as we venture into the next section, it's knowledge that empowers us to make these discerning choices.

The Ever-Evolving Power of Knowledge

Knowledge is not merely information—it's power. Rooted in the theory of tabula rasa, humans are said to begin life as a blank canvas, void of innate ideas. As we grow, we absorb lessons from our environments, guided by familial patterns. When I was a child, I loved my family but the lack of engagement and my boredom often drove me to seek more. It wasn't just about letting kids be kids. The under-stimulation of my early years pushed me away from my hometown.

The phrase, "Let kids be kids" was frequently echoed in my Ohio upbringing. The saying seems to champion a period of life characterized by playfulness, little responsibility, and freedom from adult concerns. Yet, if adults wistfully look back on these supposedly golden years as better than their current lives—times when they were less educated, lacked discipline, and were largely powerless—it raises questions about our societal values.

In truth, the notion that childhood is inherently superior to adulthood is a misconception. Children, limited in both knowledge and autonomy, navigate life with a kind of blissful ignorance that, while endearing, is hardly a recipe for long-term well-being or success. The sentimentality for a carefree childhood can blind us to the opportunities we have for meaningful engagement and education from an early age. Rather than a life stage to be nostalgically cherished, childhood can be a crucial time for comprehensive development—physically, emotionally, and intellectually. Thus, filling these formative years with more than idle play could set the groundwork for a fulfilling, empowered life.

Our early ancestors learned through observation, imitation, and trial-and-error; their knowledge was passed down within tribal communities. *Homo habilis*, for example, learned hunting techniques by studying successful hunters. Observational learning served humans well even before the advent of language. Language, however, took human learning to a new level—enabling complex thought, problem-solving, and the transfer of information.

Artistic endeavors like cave art changed knowledge transfer from real-time, person to person, to a medium that was durable across generations. While the exact reasons behind the human evolution of learning beyond grunting and observational learning remain uncertain, theories like Charles Darwin's "pre-adaptation" (now known as "exaptation") suggest our ancestors leveraged new adaptations for unforeseen advantages. This concept suggests that a species utilizes an adaptation, such as an increased number of neurons to support a larger body, for a purpose other than its original function.

I cannot doubt that language owes its origin to the imitation and
modification, aided by signs and gestures, of various natural sounds,
the voices of other animals, and man's own instinctive cries.
— Charles Darwin, *The Descent of Man*[2]

Knowledge used to be passed down directly and inefficiently, with the human brain serving as a conduit for observational learning across multiple species and generations. That changed with the invention of language and writing, as well as the advent of technology, which has granted us unprecedented access to collective human wisdom.

Consider my third child, born in 2004. Growing up surrounded by tech-savvy siblings, he was naturally exposed to various forms of technology from a young age. While I spent my idle childhood hours in traditional games, he navigated digital worlds, grappling with on-screen text that advanced his reading skills faster than traditional methods could. By high school, he achieved a perfect score on the PSAT, a feat I attribute to his early and ongoing engagement with technology.

However, technology's impact isn't universally positive. Concerns abound over its potential harms, such as eyestrain, attention deficits, and even mental health issues. Yet, its learning potential can't be ignored. Unlike parents or caregivers, technology is always "on," offering consistent educational experiences. Moreover, emerging studies hint at a potential uptick in cognitive capabilities linked to digital media usage, offering a more nuanced view of technology's role in human development. A few promising scientific studies, for example, show an IQ increase of 2.5 points compared to the overall average IQ over the same study period.[3]

The acquisition of knowledge has evolved over millennia—from primal observation to linguistic communication and now, digital engagement. As we stand on the shoulders of those who came before us, we must make the most of the tools at our disposal, for knowledge is, indeed, the most potent form of power.

The Mind: Between Tabula Rasa and Cognitive Mastery

The human brain is a marvel of biological engineering. Far from the "blank slate" suggested by the tabula rasa concept, it functions as a sophisticated processor, equipped to receive and interpret sensory input across a multitude of domains—from the visual and auditory to the tactile and olfactory. With its staggering network of 100 billion neurons and a quadrillion synaptic connections, the brain's capabilities defy easy comprehension.

Its true genius, perhaps, lies in its plasticity—the ability to change and adapt throughout a person's lifetime. Neuroplasticity allows for the continuous formation of new neural pathways and the reorganization of existing networks, making lifelong learning more than a possibility—it's a given.

Though we might be tempted to think of the brain as a finite storage unit, its reality is far more dynamic. It continuously restructures itself to accommodate new experiences, making room for fresh learning and understanding. Once information finds a home within its intricate network, the brain moves to organize it, clustering related data for more efficient storage and retrieval.

It's worth mentioning the phenomenon known as Miller's Law, named after cognitive psychologist George A. Miller. According to Miller, the average human's short-term memory can accommodate about seven items—be it a phone number or a list of names. Transitioning these fragments to long-term memory requires active participation. Though we cannot control this process directly, strategies like focused attention, repetition, and stress management can facilitate it.[4]

Unlike a computer hard drive, memories in the human brain are not static. They enter and exit our consciousness, triggered by external or internal cues. For example, the mere mention of your twenty-first birthday or your first car could bring those memories to the forefront of your consciousness, linking them with the experience of reading this memoir.

This interplay of neural networks, memory storage, and individual experiences culminates in what we understand as our "subjective reality." It's a unique interpretation of the world, distinct from objective truths but nonetheless real to us. This led me to grapple with a profound question: Who is in charge? Is it my brain that controls me, or do I have control over it? And if my brain governs my physical actions, what does it mean for my thoughts and my consciousness? The implications of this question can be as fascinating as they are disconcerting.

I ENCOUNTERED MANY OPPORTUNITIES, challenges, distractions, and successes that shaped my unique reality. Society and the pressure to fit in played a significant role, pushing me to become a productive member of the system. Although my drive wasn't solely focused on success, my competitiveness compelled me to outperform my peers. Amidst the pursuit of jobs, relationships, and family, my desire for happiness often took a backseat.

However, in 2010, the tragic death of Scott Birk planted the seed of doubt in my mind, making me realize that I may not have full control over my own life. There was a profound connection between his fate and my own future. Then, in 2011, my oldest daughter made the decision to finish high school in Ohio, leaving Texas. Though beyond my control, her absence continues to impact me. In 2016, my then-wife initiated a divorce, and I agreed without hesitation.

Throughout those years, my unhappiness grew. The divorce forced me to reevaluate my life. While it relieved one emotional burden, it brought chaos and significant changes for both of us. Selling the home where I raised my children felt like hitting rock bottom. However, amidst the turmoil, a glimmer of hope emerged—a fresh start without the weight of a relationship. A lifetime of experiences had shaped the unhappy successful man I had become.

Like Mark Doran's question to me so many years ago, I asked myself: What do you want to do with your life, John? Again, I mostly could only identify what I didn't want. I knew I no longer wanted to be married. I knew I did not want to continue working in a sales job for corporate America. One thing I knew I wanted more of was the happiness I felt while riding my bicycle.

The Crossroads: Unraveling Success and Fulfillment

My life's been shaped by all sorts of things—grabbing opportunities, facing down challenges, dodging distractions, and racking up some wins. Society and the pressure to fit in pushed me toward being an industrious cog in the system. Driven by a competitive streak, I spent years trying to climb social and professional ladders. But while I was busy chasing my career, dealing with work pressures, and family-related issues, I neglected my own happiness.

Milestones like the untimely death of Scott Birk, my oldest daughter moving away for school, and a painful divorce served as wake-up calls, making me reassess my priorities. The divorce, while painful, offered a fresh start. I began focusing on small joys, like solitary moments for self-reflection and the sense of accomplishment from cycling. Friendships with people like Hollie Kenney, a fantastic friend to this day, offered new perspectives and helped chip away at the long-standing unhappiness that had defined me.

THE FASTEST LABOR DAY EVER

*"One of the most important days of my life, was when I learned
to ride a bicycle."*
— Michael Palin

VASE to ZYGO.

The value of secondhand stories shouldn't be underestimated.
They offer us glimpses into lives and events we haven't personally
experienced, broadening our worldview and enriching our understanding of various situations. These tales can serve as warnings,
allowing us to glean important lessons without enduring the same
hardships ourselves. They give us the privilege to learn from others'
errors, triumphs, or challenges.

Yet, there's no substitute for firsthand experiences. They possess
an emotional and sensory intensity that far exceeds the confines of
any narrative. The act of physically engaging with the world around
us, feeling the impact of choices and consequences in real-time,
has an unparalleled force.

For three years following Scott's tragic accident, I couldn't shake
off the memory of it, especially when I ran past the intersection
where his life was cut short. But only two years had passed when I
found myself dashing across that same road without waiting for the
WALK signal. I hadn't forgotten the lesson; instead, I had become

more vigilant. I reasoned that with heightened alertness, I could beat the odds and cross safely, shaving a few precious minutes off my run. The raw fear of potential injury had diminished, but the possibility of danger never vanished.

And so, I continued my twin passions of running and biking, albeit more cautiously than before. But then, one pivotal morning in 2016, life decided to underscore just how swiftly our perspective can turn, and how our reality can be upended in the blink of an eye.

A Turn of Events: From Routine to Revelation

Labor Day 2016 started as a day of anticipation. Fresh off a week-long Caribbean cruise—replete with luxurious meals—I was eager to burn some serious calories. I had signed up for the Fastest Labor Day Ever, a sixty-mile cycling event hosted by Bat City Cycling Club (BCCC), one of Austin's most established cycling teams. It promised to be more than just a workout; it was an event.

The dawn of Labor Day saw me wide awake, tingling with a mix of eagerness and jitters for the ride that lay ahead. When my alarm rang at 6:30 AM, I quickly got out of bed. As I did, an odd sensation gripped me—the floor felt like it was moving, a lingering effect from my recent cruise known as mal de debarquement. It was an amusing, if slightly disorienting, start to the day.

Group rides had always been fun, offering a chance to push my physical limits amidst an eclectic group of cyclists with varying skills and fitness. This was much different from the indoor Spin classes I typically led as an instructor.

Cycling meetups often start in coffee shops—a casual prelude to the main event. However, when these seemingly leisurely rides are organized by avid cyclists like the BCCC, the laid-back pace morphs into something more adrenaline-fueled. It becomes a test of speed, strength, and stamina.

Veterans like Vince Marotte, a BCCC mainstay, have their capabilities well-known within the community. For relative newcomers like me, the initial stretch is all about gauging one's fitness and securing a comfortable spot in the peloton. Though not the fastest, my extensive endurance training in running and cycling gave me the stamina to gradually nudge toward the front of the pack.

Arriving at the Red Horn Coffee House and Brewing Co., the designated starting point, I felt a surge of excitement as I unloaded my bike. About fifty riders milled around, prepping their gear. Recognizable faces were few; I'd only cycled with this group on a couple of occasions.

As the air buzzed with anticipation, a voice rang out: "Let's have a fast and safe ride." The last memory I have was clicking into my pedals, exiting the parking lot, and taking a sharp right turn onto Parmer Lane. Unbeknownst to me, this ride would take a profoundly unexpected turn. Around thirty minutes in, I was involved in a severe accident, a life-defining moment that shifted the entire focus of my world—and this book.

Mile 13 – A Mile Unlike Any Other

In an orchestrated ballet of motion, we cyclists rode two abreast, each pair maintaining a space of twelve to twenty-four inches between their bikes. We occupied the shoulder of the road, the looming highway barrier hugging our right side. We were a living, breathing entity, a tightly-knit unit moving in unison, heads down and legs pumping. Weeks later, the details of what unfolded would be relayed back to me. According to the accounts of my fellow riders, by the time we hit the thirteenth mile on Ronald Reagan Boulevard in Georgetown, Texas, I was situated toward the rear third of our group.

Some ten riders ahead of me was Tom Lawrence, a BCCC veteran known for his astounding annual tally of over 10,000 miles. As we approached the midpoint of a bridge, calamity struck. Tom's front tire collided with a stray piece of metal, immediately bursting and sending him careening to the asphalt below. The resulting impact fractured his clavicle, scapula, eight ribs, and punctured his lung. Astonishingly, all this devastation occurred from what appeared to be a trivial three-foot fall, but at an incredible speed of thirty miles per hour.

The fallout from Tom's crash rippled through our ranks. Alert riders, in an adrenaline-fueled instant, braked and swerved to prevent a pile-up. Navigating instinctually, I steered rightward, grazing the road's edge. In doing so, I successfully stopped my bike and avoided any collisions with fellow cyclists.

But coming to such an abrupt stop had its own peril. The angular momentum that normally keeps a cyclist upright had vanished in an instant. My Garmin 910XT GPS watch clocked me at nearly thirty miles per hour before my speed hit zero. Sandwiched between my fellow cyclists and the low-lying highway barrier, I found my balance wavering dangerously. Cyclists like me use specialized cleated shoes that lock into clipless pedals, enhancing our connection to the bike but making quick disengagement tricky. In a crisis, I've often lifted my foot straight up, the wrong move, rather than twisting it to unlock from the pedal, resulting in falls.

As I teetered, I began to topple toward the barrier which served as an unintended fulcrum, instigating a clockwise spin of both me and my bike. Witnesses say we reached for each other, but events transpired too swiftly for our hands to meet. Though I have no memory of this, the horror those riders must have felt watching me plummet off the bridge is unimaginable.

I plunged fifty feet to the ground below, landing on a bed of rock and earth. No eyes followed me down; what happened next is deduced from the injuries I sustained. In those two fleeting seconds of free fall, I executed a clockwise rotation before crashing into the ground at an astonishing forty miles per hour. Remarkably, I landed wheels-first, tilted slightly to the right—a detail that unquestionably saved my life.

My bike, crafted from carbon fiber, bore the initial brunt of the impact, its rear wheel splintering upon collision. My right pedal also snapped, further diffusing the impact force. As I hit the ground, elements of carbon fiber, metal, flesh, and bone compressed against the unforgiving rocky surface below. How long I lay there, motionless, is a mystery, but one thing is abundantly clear: had I landed any other way, I would not have survived.

Angels on Wheels

Word of the crash and my fall from the bridge spread like wildfire through the scattered peloton. Swiftly, several cyclists doubled back to the incident spot. Abandoning their bikes, they ran to the bridge approach, hurriedly descended the rocky slope, and rushed to reach me. They remained by my side for the vital twenty to thirty minutes that elapsed before emergency responders and a helicopter arrived on the scene.

Christie Tracy, Seth Williams, and Dave Aronson were some of the first to arrive, although my memory of these events remains a blank. I finally got to hear Christie's viewpoint in a conversation two and a half years after the incident. An elite athlete, Christie won the "Time Trial 12-Hour World Champion" title in 2017 by cycling an astounding 248 miles at an average speed of 20.8 miles per hour.

On that fateful day, Christie was positioned ahead of the accident, but the unmistakable cacophony of a crash prompted her to swing her bike around and rush back. "I know the sound of a crash all too well—bikes scraping and carbon fiber breaking," she recounted. "It is the worst feeling; you do not want to look back, but you know you have to."

The scene she arrived at was disarrayed, with damaged bikes and injured riders sprawled across the asphalt. Tom, whose tire puncture triggered the chain of events, lay on the ground in agony. "I felt a spike of adrenaline when I saw him," Christie explained, "and several cyclists were already helping him." Just then, someone mentioned a guy had gone over the side of the bridge.

"I could not process what I heard. It seemed unreal. It felt like ten minutes when it was probably ten seconds before I could react," Christie said, recalling her sprint toward the bridge's edge.

"I thought, 'get down there as quickly as you can,' and a whole lot of 'no no no no nos.'"

The descent was slippery and hazardous in cycling shoes, but driven by adrenaline, she made it to the ground beneath the bridge. "No one on the bridge thought you survived the fall, but when I got down there, I found you in the one soft spot surrounded by unforgiving rock," she told me.

Upon arrival, two cyclists I have not been able to identify were already by my side when Christie and Seth Williams reached the scene. Christie described her initial impressions: "At first glance, I saw that you were breathing and then you started to slowly regain consciousness. After a couple of moments, you wanted to move and you were very agitated. I could see you were broken. Your right elbow bone was sticking out and the wound was open. The only way I can describe it is to say that it looked like a ham hock."

She continued, "You kept trying to move and wanted to take your helmet off. I was attempting to distract you from your injuries, from the bicycle, from everything. You were disoriented, insistent on standing up as if you were fine. You mentioned that your leg was starting to hurt, and you wanted to roll over, but we restrained you. We were all concerned about potential back injuries and the risks of any sudden movements."

"You ripped off your helmet... Logical reasoning wasn't getting through to you. I assumed your head was in pain and that you wanted the helmet off. Perhaps your brain was swelling; you had a cut on your forehead, so maybe the impact from the rock was causing the discomfort. You were speaking, but your words were jumbled. You couldn't grasp the gravity of your condition or what had happened to you."

"It felt like an eternity waiting for the EMTs and the helicopter to arrive. Whenever you tried to move, I would ask you unrelated questions to distract you. While the EMT was attending to you, I kept talking. We searched your shirt pockets for identification or a phone; we found your iPhone, miraculously intact, but locked."

"I couldn't believe that you were still alive . . . that you were alive and breathing . . . I can't put into words the emotions. As I stood there, thoughts flooded my mind—'Oh God, oh shit'—wondering, what kind of future lay ahead of you after such a fall."

My gratitude towards Christie is beyond measure. She jeopardized her own well-being to come down from that bridge and offer assistance. Her quick thinking and empathy most likely saved my life. Once a stranger, she is now a hero in my life.

ANOTHER PERSON WHO HAS become a hero in my life is **Kyle McKnight**, the first certified paramedic from Williamson County EMS to arrive on the scene. We met in person for the first time on January 11, 2018, a year and a half post-accident, outside a hospital setting. During our conversation, Kyle detailed the mechanics of my rescue.

On the day of the accident, Kyle was stationed in Florence, Texas He immediately responded to the emergency call in Squad 30, a Chevy Tahoe equipped for Advanced Life Support. Unlike a standard ambulance, this lighter, four-wheel-drive vehicle with high clearance was ideal for rural terrains, allowing for better maneuverability. En route, Kyle proactively put an air ambulance on standby, a decision that would later prove crucial in reducing response time.

Upon reaching the bridge, Kyle quickly assessed the situation. Finding no critical injuries among the cyclists on the bridge, he focused on reaching me—the rider who had fallen off the bridge. He adeptly maneuvered the Tahoe down the rugged, rocky slope to where I lay. Upon exiting the vehicle, he quickly gathered the necessary medical equipment. Prepared to encounter a fatality due to the severity of the fall, Kyle was surprised to learn from my fellow cyclists—Christie, Seth, and Dave—that I was still breathing and able to speak.

His rapid initial assessment of my condition considered the multitude of risks associated with a fall from such a height—concussions, severe fractures, internal injuries, even fatality. However, he found me surprisingly intact, displaying only minimal blood loss but showing signs of disorientation and confusion.

Realizing the critical nature of the situation, Kyle immediately requested air medical transport, aware that every second in the "golden hour" after a traumatic incident was crucial for survival. The Level II Trauma Center at Seton Medical Center Williamson was located nineteen miles away. Simultaneously, he monitored my deteriorating condition. My frequent utterances of "I have to pee" alarmed him, as it could signify internal bleeding and brain damage.

Given my critically low blood pressure, Kyle surmised internal bleeding. To elevate my blood pressure without the benefit of a transfusion, he opted for a saline IV, despite its potential drawbacks. Stabilizing my condition was necessary before transport. He also took steps to immobilize my neck and spine and to wrap my visibly fractured elbow.

Faced with the difficult decision of whether to administer pain medication, which could lower my already critical blood pressure, Kyle opted to keep me conscious. He confided in me later, "I know I'd want to be knocked out if I was in your situation, but keeping you awake proved beneficial." During the transfer to the helicopter landing zone, I was able to tell him about my difficulty breathing. Instantly recognizing the symptom of a collapsed lung due to internal bleeding, he halted the transfer. Without wasting time, Kyle performed an emergency thoracentesis by using a large needle to drain fluid from my chest. This swift action alleviated the pressure around my lungs, allowing them to fully expand. Had I been unconscious, this crucial communication wouldn't have been possible. By the time we made it to the roadway, the landing area was already secured by the local Florence Volunteer Fire Department, and the helicopter was prepped for immediate takeoff.

As we flew to the hospital, my Garmin GPS watch, still strapped to my wrist, recorded the details of the journey, marking a fifteen-mile flight reaching a top speed of 119 miles per hour, that took a remarkable nine minutes.

Weeks later, while transporting another patient to the same hospital, Kyle learned of my survival. Astonished, he visited me. Though my recollection of those initial post-accident days is fuzzy, his visit stands out, captured forever in a photograph.

When we had the opportunity to reunite in January 2018, Kyle's face lit up as he watched me walk toward the coffee table. My own sense of curiosity was piqued; I was eager to hear his account of the fateful day. Kyle generously filled in the gaps in my understanding, offering critical details about the accident that I hadn't known. As we delved into memories of our first meeting in the hospital back in 2016, he recalled telling me, "Let's go for a bike ride when you get out of here." He admitted that the words left his mouth before he had the chance to consider the uphill battle I faced in recovery, not to mention the uncertainty of whether I'd ever be able to cycle again.

Later that year, Kyle sponsored my attendance at the Williamson County Paramedic EMS annual awards reception. It was a momentous occasion where I had the chance to publicly thank Kyle and his colleagues for their lifesaving work, acknowledging both the victories and losses inherent to their profession. I stressed a point that was self-evident yet powerful: "While survivors like me have the privilege to offer thanks, those who aren't as fortunate can't express their gratitude. My heartfelt thanks for all that you do."

To Kyle and emergency responders everywhere, I owe a debt of gratitude. Their dedication and expertise give people like me not just a second chance at life, but the potential for a fulfilled one.

An Observer's View from Behind

Dave Aronson, out cycling with his spouse at the time, observed the unfolding event as the BCCC group passed by them on Ronald Reagan Boulevard before arriving at the bridge. He later chronicled his direct experience of the incident on Facebook:

. . . a group of riders passed us. Moments later, there was an accident, a horrible accident. The rider in front had a blowout and crashed, next thing we see is a rider fly over the barrier on the bridge and fall fifty feet onto limestone.

Most were in shock, and my co-worker Seth Williams got down to him to help him. I called 911, started directing traffic and someone called for someone who knew CPR. I raced down thinking the worst. I was surprised I was the only one trained in CPR and First Aid. When I got down there, the rider was lying in a crumpled ball Bones exposed through his skin, blood, helmet crushed, glasses crushed.

He was alive somehow, in incredible pain and not making a lot of sense. Seth Williams is holding him still and talking with him. He remains incredibly calm. It was horrible, he didn't need CPR, but it was amazing he was still alive. How could this really be happening . . . Paramedics finally show up after what felt like forever. I meet them at the top of the hill and help carry bags to the victim. The paramedic is shocked he is still alive, told the victim John later that he thought he was going to see a dead body. They take his BP and there is no BP. It is bad, really bad. Lung collapses and they re-inflate it as they carry him off. After what seems like forever the helicopter arrives and takes him away . . . We think the worst.

Seth checks in with him a few days later and he is living. No way he will ride again, no way he will ever walk again . . . Major head injuries, no clue what happened.

Defying The Odds

Surviving a fall from fifty feet is nothing short of a medical marvel; the survival rate is below one percent. Yet, at each crucial juncture, from the immediate EMS response to the rapid helicopter evacuation and specialized trauma care, my chances incrementally improved.

Trauma centers are rated Level I through V based on their service capabilities. I was lucky to be near a Level II facility. The trauma team's initial evaluation was vital. They had advanced notice of my internal bleeding from the EMTs, which was corroborated by my low blood pressure, lack of external injuries, a collapsed lung, and abdominal distension. This signaled immediate action—a massive transfusion protocol was initiated, aiming to first stabilize me for ensuing treatments.

As the surgeons conducted an exploratory laparotomy, where an eight-inch midline incision was made from just under my sternum toward my navel, they discovered a hemoperitoneum—blood pooling in the abdominal cavity—signifying a ruptured superior mesenteric artery. A deeper examination revealed a dissection of my aorta's inner layer, an extremely dangerous condition that can lead to almost instant death. An aortic dissection occurs when blood penetrates the inner layer and accumulates between the layers. With adept surgical intervention, an aortic arch stent graft was implanted to stabilize the aorta.

Once stable, focus shifted to my shattered right femur. A small incision below the knee allowed for a sixteen-inch titanium rod to be placed inside the femur, secured at each end with screws. The titanium was designed to be stronger than the bone it replaced. My doctor later confided in me, "Our primary goal was to save your life, even if that meant we couldn't address everything at once." He expressed concerns that the rapid pace of the emergency interventions might necessitate additional treatments in the future, like bone grafts.

The impact also resulted in an 'open-book' pelvic fracture, splitting my pelvis. To realign and secure the two halves, two ten-inch upper screws and a lower chain with five additional screws were used. Months later, when I saw my X-ray, it intriguingly resembled a bike chain, an unexpected connection between the incident and my love of cycling.

While my bicycle helmet shielded much of my head, the region just above my eyebrows and beneath my hairline remained exposed. The impact with the rocky surface led to a Traumatic Brain Injury (TBI), specifically identified as brain shear. The full scope of this injury wasn't apparent to the doctors until a few days had passed. For the initial four days, I was heavily sedated, reliant on life support, and semi-conscious. Yet, I could still execute basic commands and indicate pain through finger movements.

By the fourth day, I was only able to say my name after the breathing tube was removed, but my cognitive functions began to decline in the days that followed. Medical records describe my mental state as increasingly confused and distressed. A nurse noted a few days later, "However, in the last day or two, he has had a decompensation of his mentation. He is acutely distressed. He is groaning. He is moaning. He is awake. He is oriented to his first name. When I asked to hold up two fingers on his left hand, he was able to do that. When I asked him if he was in pain, he said yes. Otherwise, he did not respond to any questions."

Subsequent MRI spectroscopy unveiled the existence of brain shear, a condition where the brain's elongated nerve fibers tear due to internal movements of the brain within the skull. This level of TBI can result in enduring changes to one's physical, emotional, cognitive, and behavioral health. It's worth noting that about half of TBI sufferers may face diminished daily functionality or increased mortality risk within five years following the incident.

My brother, who held my medical power of attorney, later admitted to me that he had braced himself for the possibility of my memory loss becoming irreversible. However, the brain's exceptional ability to adapt, change, and rewire itself—even after severe trauma—cannot be underestimated. Unbeknownst to me at that moment were the immense hurdles lying ahead, hurdles that would test my resolve and resilience.

ACCIDENTAL MOTIVATION

"Adversity introduces a man to himself."
— Albert Einstein

The Philosophical Awakening: September 5, 2016

A life philosophy is more than just a set of intellectual ideas; it's a guide that shapes our understanding of the world, our sense of purpose, our ethics, and our experience as human beings. This philosophy becomes the foundation for our values and choices, helping us find our way through the complexities of life. While some spend years pondering and shaping their belief systems, mine was sparked by a single, pivotal event: the bike accident on September 5, 2016. This critical moment launched me on a philosophical quest and offered me a renewed opportunity to seek genuine happiness.

The Dream and the Reality of TBI

Traumatic Brain Injury (TBI) doesn't just rob you of your physical abilities, it distorts the very fabric of your memory and consciousness. In the aftermath of my accident, I was caught in a fog of medical interventions—life support switches, anesthesia, surgeries, and an array of visits from loved ones. All these occurrences were later recounted to me, filling in the gaps of what I could not remember. During the twelve days that immediately followed the accident, my conscious memory was limited to one surreal experience: a vivid dream.

The dream transported me back to a setting that was all too familiar. There I was, basking in the Caribbean sun, meandering along the expansive top deck of a luxury cruise ship. I had just returned from a similar vacation two days before my accident, so the scene was comfortingly recognizable. The deck was a buzzing hub of activity, complete with pools, lounges, and the merry clinking of cocktail glasses. But as I descended the staircase, a jarring transition began to unfold. The vibrant potted plants along the deck gave way to cold metal, the ship's teak stairs morphed into diamond-gripped treads, and an oppressive sense of dread filled the air.

Suddenly, I found myself in a dystopian reality. I was no longer on a luxury liner; instead, I stood on a container ship. In a desperate attempt to make sense of this shift, I approached a door leading into the ship's dark interior. Peering through the porthole, I encountered a haunting scene that could have been lifted straight from the thriller "Coma," released in 1978 and remade in 2012. I saw rows upon rows of human bodies, suspended from the ceiling, ventilated and immobile.

In the blink of an eye, the observer became the observed. I was one of those bodies: trapped, intubated, my freedom taken from me. It was a nightmarish limbo where time lost all meaning, lasting both an instant and an eternity.

The Fog of Forgotten Faces

My post-amnestic recovery began on September 17, 2016. Although I began to be able to recall specific memories, my brain was in the midst of a significant reboot. I would recognize faces but couldn't place the names or how I knew them. Pieces of my past would come back to me, but they seemed disconnected from my current situation. I could answer basic questions like my name or where I was, but then would quickly forget, which was incredibly frustrating.

One defining episode stands out, albeit only through others recounting it to me. On the twelfth day, my former wife visited the

ICU, her face igniting a dim spark of recognition in me. She relayed this to our children and quickly returned with them, marking a hopeful yet tenuous milestone for our family. My son later told me that despite this glimmer of recognition, doubts persisted regarding the scope of my eventual recovery. My physical state—a face marred by cuts and bruises, a body swathed in bandages—added to their fear and uncertainty.

Those initial days with my family remain in a cloud of oblivion. My children tested my mental faculties with simple questions like what's your name, where is home, and how many siblings do you have, to which I could only offer fragments of vague memories. It wasn't until days later, when my short-term memory started functioning that I first remember hearing, "You were in an accident."

The Rebirth: A Parallel Universe Unveiled

For nearly two weeks after my accident, I lived in a world devoid of self-awareness, in a state of global amnesia. The first memory fragments that I could recall after the fourteenth day were disjointed and dreamlike, pulling me into a parallel universe of sorts. The earliest memory was like my mother's voice waking me for elementary school—a gentle, comforting voice assuring me, "Everything is fine. You're in the hospital." Visitors spoke to me about someone who had experienced a horrific accident but linking that individual to my current self did not make sense. Even though physical scars provided evidence, a part of my mind seemed to question their relevance to me.

Confined to a hospital bed and surrounded by a maze of medical equipment, I was immobilized both physically and mentally. Cut off from the treasury of memories that used to define me, I discovered an unusual clarity in that isolation. I felt freed from past desires, goals, and relationships.

The irony was hard to miss: the person I was in the hospital had no memory of the accident thus the person who had fallen off the bridge was gone; in his place was the new me. A person who knew only of a hospital room and scattered bits of awareness.

My mind was like a blank slate. I had no memory of being a dad, an athlete, or someone with a career. Each moment stood alone as the only reality I knew. As family and friends shared stories about my past, it felt as though they were talking about a different person. Their memories became my only link to who I used to be, though it felt like I was borrowing someone else's life story.

In the weeks after I started remembering things again, I had to live completely in the moment. This was different from the kind of mindfulness you hear about in Buddhism, Taoism, or Stoicism. In those traditions, people choose to focus only on the present, letting go of thoughts about the past or future. My situation was different; I didn't have a choice. Because I had lost my memories, I was forced into a kind of extreme focus on the present. The past had no influence on me, and I couldn't think about the future.

Visits from friends were a blur, due to both brain injury and medication. It's both touching and disheartening that numerous people visited me during a time my brain was unable to retain memories. Jump to 2023, and a casual catch-up with a friend took an unexpected turn. "You looked right at us and said, 'I know you,' even though you couldn't remember our names," he reflected. All I could say was, "I don't remember your visit." Others, like Christie Tracy and Seth Williams—who were part of the bike ride on the day of my accident—also came to see me during my first twelve days in the hospital. They left their contact information, realizing that I might not remember their visit or support during that crucial time.

When Tom Lawrence visited me in the hospital, I didn't recognize him. Only later did he share the specifics of the accident and our first meeting. "I was horrified to hear someone had fallen off the bridge," Tom said. After he had been discharged from the hospital and undergone his own surgery, he felt an urge to visit me. "When I walked into your hospital room, I was overcome with emotion. You were in terrible shape," he recounted. He introduced himself and told me, "I was part of the accident too. A blowout on my tire set off the whole chain of events." As he said this, tears filled his eyes, prompting tears from me as well. We embraced, each overwhelmed with gratitude for still being alive. Even though I had no recollection of our initial, emotional meeting, hearing about it later became an unforgettable part of my memory.

WHILE I FELT THE weight of loneliness, the effort required to interact with visitors often felt overwhelming. I appreciated the quiet presence of my friend, Hollie Kenney, yet I struggled with intermittent bouts of depression, which were fueled by my restricted mobility and isolation. Yet, even small milestones, like holding a fork for the first time post-accident, uplifted my spirits, offering glimmers of hope in a grim reality.

Sitting by my side in the hospital, Hollie, a fitness trainer and former pro triathlete, posed a thought-provoking question: "What do you want to do once you're out of here? Climb Mount Kilimanjaro?"

Lying there with my pelvis in two pieces, metal rods and plates holding various bones together, and both arms immobilized, I looked out the window and pondered her question. All I could think was, "I just want to walk again." At that moment, I didn't know how this simple goal would set the stage for the boundaries of my own recovery and achievements.

Was my goal too humble? Did Hollie see a greater potential in me? Perhaps it was a mix of both. As I dealt with constant pain, my aim was straightforward, if uncertain.

Goals have the power to transform lives by providing focus, demanding dedication, and instilling a sense of purpose. Hollie is adept at steering people toward ambitious objectives. On March 16, 2018, she achieved a remarkable feat by summiting Mount Kilimanjaro with her young daughter, Montannah. At just seven years old—or 2,865 days—Montannah set a world record as the youngest girl to reach the peak.

Yet, an old piece of advice from my twenties echoed in my mind: "Don't tell me what you don't want to do. Tell me what you do want to do." I realized just making it through each day wasn't enough; I needed a plan for happiness.

Accepting Help and Finding Gratitude

In the first few weeks after the accident, I really needed help. My left arm didn't work for three weeks, my legs for two months, and my right arm for six months. I used to think I could do everything on my own, but I found out I couldn't.

In a society that cherishes self-reliance, the need to depend on others was a humbling pivot. I had always taken care of everything in my life—education, relationships, finances—on my own. Yet, confined to my bed and relying on others for even the most basic tasks, a crucial insight emerged. Interdependence was not a flaw or a sign of weakness; it was, in fact, a fundamental building block of community.

Learning to accept help, starting with the hospital staff, I grew comfortable letting people into my life. The kindness of others overwhelmed me, like when I offhandedly mentioned craving a chocolate shake and visitors kept bringing them. Each chocolate shake felt like an unexpected gift. Being more open didn't just make me happier; it also made the people around me feel better and helped improve our friendships.

Before the accident, I was stubborn and prided myself on self-reliance. But going through this life-changing experience made me see the importance of community. I came to understand that we're all connected in some way, a lesson that was tough to learn but will serve me well for the rest of my life. Surviving against the odds filled me with a deep sense of gratitude for life itself. I started to value every moment, every experience, and every person I met.

This shift in perspective didn't just reinforce what I already believed; it spurred me to take action. I coined the term "accidental motivation" to describe the newfound drive that pushed me to appreciate all aspects of life, both good and bad. This also encouraged me to work on becoming the best version of myself. With this new mindset, I focused on building deeper and more meaningful relationships with people.

Overall, my viewpoint changed dramatically, heightening my awareness of my own thoughts, feelings, and the world around me. Though the accident forced me into a new chapter of my life that I didn't choose, I decided to seize this unexpected opportunity to live more fully.

At thirty-seven, I had already lived longer than my father. At fifty-two, laying in my hospital bed in 2016, memories of my father surfaced. I was just a child of ten when he left this world, depriving me of countless future moments—like playing catch, hearing the sound of his trumpet, watching his fingers dance across the accordion, playing piano, or finishing that Pinewood Derby car we had started but never completed. These memories were a poignant reminder of a bond severed too soon, a bond whose absence has reverberated throughout my life.

When the accident occurred, my son John August was eleven, unsettlingly close to the age I was when I lost my own father. This chilling coincidence evoked feelings of loss and the dread of what could have been. My mind was flooded with visions of John August enduring the painful void that I knew all too well. The thought of him missing out on years of shared experiences and memories with me was profoundly distressing.

MY RECOLLECTION ABOUT MY twenty-three-day stay in the hospital is pretty short because those days are kind of a blur. I had no memory for fourteen days, then my cognitive recovery was just beginning, so a lot of what happened is just not clear in my mind. Plus, I was on medication that made me sleep a lot. I only remember a few visitors like family members, and I was so out of it that I even started taking pictures of nurses' and doctors' nametags just to remember who they were. It was a confusing time, and writing about it in detail would be hard because my memories are so scattered. This short section actually captures how disjointed and hazy that whole hospital experience was for me.

Transition to Brookdale Nursing Facility

Moving to the Brookdale skilled nursing facility on September 27, 2016, was a roller-coaster of an experience. I was forced to leave the hospital and move to Brookdale due to insurance restrictions, even though I was far from fully healed. Being transferred on the flat ambulance cot was a new and unsettling experience for me. I felt as vulnerable as a fragile package being carefully handled for delivery, intensifying my sense of helplessness. Amid the chaos, however, there was a moment of respite. Being wheeled outside for the first time in nearly a month, I felt the sun on my face, and for a brief instant, I felt truly alive.

The initial week at Brookdale had its share of ups and downs. Obstacles with insurance paperwork made for a rocky start, but the commencement of physical therapy brought a fleeting sense of optimism. This optimism was short-lived, however, as my therapy was denied coverage by insurance due to my inability to support weight on my legs. I had to wait two weeks to start therapy, pending approval from Dr. Hill, my orthopedic surgeon.

The delay in therapy was more than frustrating—it meant I was stuck in bed. I took daily pain meds and had only a vague idea of how my brain injury was affecting me. Looking back, it's clear that my cognitive capabilities were seriously hampered, making the management of my own well-being and finances an added stressor. Therapy wasn't just treatment for me; it symbolized a fresh start in life. Its delay was one of the hardest times for me on my road to recovery.

Will I Ever Walk?

After the accident that wrecked my lower body, one big question haunted me: Would I ever walk again? We often take life's little conveniences for granted, hardly noticing their importance until they're gone. Before my accident, I never thought twice about walking, but the constant worry about whether I would regain this ability made even simple daily activities feel more challenging. I was caught in a mix of hope and dread, constantly questioning whether I'd ever walk again or if I could ever be the person I was before.

Hollie came to see me during that initial conscious week in the hospital, a week marked by a barrage of medical updates and procedures. Keeping tabs on all this was a logistical nightmare. Hollie, noticing my actions, suggested that I document my journey to recovery. Despite the difficulty in moving my arms, I heeded her advice and began making voice recordings on my iPhone. Oddly enough, I didn't revisit these recordings for the next six years. However, while writing this memoir, delving into these recordings revealed them to be an invaluable archive, preserving details I might have otherwise forgotten.

While at Brookdale, I also used my iPhone's voice-to-text to take notes. These fleeting thoughts found a permanent home in my Notes app, with each entry acting as a marker on my complex road to recovery.

October 17, 2016, marked a turning point: I was to find out if I could begin the much-awaited physical therapy, a crucial step toward regaining normalcy. I clearly remember the outcome of that appointment, but looking back at my notes, some are surprisingly funny and interesting. Recorded and transcribed later that same day, these are my unedited notes:

Great sleep 10:15 – 7:00. Peed 1x. Sarah A came in at 5 AM to make sure I was ok.

9:15 am **Shower** Sara Vasquez gave me a shower. Sisco took off and put on my arm brace. First wash for right foot. Lots of dead skin came off. Shaved my face too. She rubbed lotion on my arms and legs.

11:00 am, I feel tired. Weird because I slept so well.

12:45 Shelley Cawthon, Brookdale transport driver took me to Dr Hill. She said the Brookdale office gave her the wrong address. She called to confirm, and they told her what they told me – Mays Ave in Round Rock

5:30 pm got back to Brookdale. Ass hurts!

Dr Hill Comments

X-rays of pelvis, both elbows right wrist femur and ankle.

Green light to start full motion weight bearing exercises.

Left elbow – work on full extension. A little extra bone grew which is limiting motion.

Right elbow – full motion in brace during physical therapy. Don't need brace outside of physical therapy if I want.

Right wrist – there is a screw in the bone because they expected me to weight bear sooner. Work on strength and full motion. The elbow nerve wasn't cut, but it was bruised. Get a nerve test. May require transplant worst case.

Pelvis – looks good. Ok to start weight bearing.

Right Femur – it was in 3 pieces and they didn't have a lot of time because of my condition for extra screws. Middle piece isn't aligned perfectly. May require bone graft in the future. Ok for weight.

Right Ankle – ok. Work on motion. Can hang out and sleep without boot!

Oddly enough, I started making notes about when I went to the bathroom. I'm not sure why it mattered, but what became more important was keeping track of my bowel movements. I discovered through a difficult experience that the combination of my medications and prolonged bed rest could lead to severe constipation. Twice, I needed a nurse to help sort it out—a humbling experience, to say the least.

THE NEXT DAY WAS CALM until my 2 PM physical therapy appointment. Eating lunch, I felt a wave of relief knowing that Dr. Hill had okayed my insurance to cover the nursing home stay. I was over the moon when my physical therapist, Maridee Cavalida, walked in and announced, "We can start therapy!" What she did next surprised me. Instead of using the Hoyer Lift to move me, Maridee helped me slide to the bed's edge and sit up. Then, she wrapped a belt around my waist. "Time to stand," she said, grinning.

"Are you serious?" I asked, nervously. Failing at this point meant more than just falling; it could indicate that my healing wasn't progressing correctly, potentially necessitating more surgery. With my broken pelvis and titanium-reinforced femur, my worries weren't baseless. But hope won over fear.

Maridee set up a walker in front of me. "One, two, three, stand," she counted, helping me up. I was so overwhelmed, I yelled, "Oh my God!" Just writing about it now gives me chills. "Let's take some steps," she said, smiling. As I took my first steps, her assistant stood by with a wheelchair, ready to assist if necessary.

The feeling of taking those first steps six weeks after my accident transcends words—it was as if my entire being exhaled a breath I didn't know I had been holding. Each footfall reverberated through me, not just as a physical act, but as a reaffirmation of life, a testament to overcoming obstacles that seemed insurmountable. With each step, I wasn't merely moving forward physically; I was reclaiming a part of myself that I had feared was lost forever. Halfway through, I sat in the wheelchair while Maridee turned me around for the return trip. As it hit me that I was really walking, I started crying. Maridee looked surprised but quickly understood the emotional weight of the moment and comforted me.

My iPhone Notes:

10/18/16 Tuesday – First Day Full Weight Rehab
2:00 pm Maridee. 90 ft. Walked! 3 sessions

10/19/16 – Wednesday
10:00 am Maridee PT Walked down hall
and cried when I was done. 350' today.

The classic line, "Put one foot in front of the other," from the song in the 1970 Christmas TV special "Santa Claus Is Comin' to Town," became my recovery mantra. In just one week, I progressed from a few shaky steps to walking an impressive 700 feet. Maridee and Anthony, my rehab therapists, were thrilled when I was able to venture outside for the first time. By the end of October, I was slowly but surely conquering stairs, a feat that left Maridee amazed considering the extent of my injuries.

Another triumph that moved me to tears was when, after months of relying on bedpans and urine bottles, I was finally able to manage the mundane yet significant task of using the toilet on my own. With my walker for support and a handrail on the wall, I lowered myself onto the toilet. Feeling a wave of joy and gratitude as I went to the bathroom unaided for the first time in what felt like forever, I vowed never to underestimate this simple act again. It was a quiet milestone, like riding a bike for the first time without training wheels, and in that sterile bathroom, it was monumental.

Connections and Reflections

During my days at Brookdale, the atmosphere often felt monotonous, almost as if the days were blending into one another. But every so often, a welcome disruption would come in the form of cards, letters, or even gift baskets. These small tokens buoyed my spirits, providing much-needed emotional uplifts.

Scheduled visits from friends and family were always a highlight, but there was something uniquely exhilarating about an unexpected knock on the door. Whoever it was, their first question was almost always, "Am I interrupting?" My answer was a resounding, "Come on in!" In an instant, the TV would be muted, any podcast paused, and my phone set aside. A quick sweep of my hand would straighten the bed sheets as I attempted to tidy up my appearance, my face beaming with genuine happiness at their presence.

In the aftermath of my accident, something incredible happened to my relationships. It's as if the visible, life-altering injuries I sustained broke down barriers and allowed for a different kind of intimacy with those who came to visit me. Bonds I had with family and friends prior to the accident took on a new dimension. The people who came to see me seemed to feel a deeper connection, a sense of shared experience that made them more willing to open up about their own struggles and challenges.

For instance, I'll never forget the day a friend showed up unexpectedly with a chocolate shake in hand. What made this visit special wasn't just the shake, though I was incredibly grateful for that, but the conversation that ensued. My friend shared a dark chapter in his life where he had seriously considered ending it all. His openness created a poignant moment that forever deepened our connection. It was as if my situation had provided a safe space for him to be vulnerable, not to gain sympathy but to genuinely relate to what I was going through.

Interacting with my family at Brookdale had a different feel compared to our interactions at the hospital. The setting was less clinical, providing opportunities for us to gather in common spaces or even venture outside. One night, close to the end of my stay, I had the incredible experience of dining out with my kids. Just getting to the car with the support of a cane was emotionally overwhelming. Yet, the seemingly simple act of settling into the car was an unexpected challenge, a reminder that my body had yet to fully recover.

I came to realize that my interactions with friends, old and new, and my family became more authentic and deeper. Moreover, my reliance on others for my most basic needs sparked an interest in me to examine how I could give back or return favors to people in my life. When I was finally able to drive again in February 2017, I acted on my newfound urge. One of the individuals I reached out to was a fellow cyclist who had been hit by a car, and another was a friend's son who was diagnosed with bone cancer during his freshman year of college. Connecting with them and offering my support not only gave me a sense of fulfillment, but I felt a connection that I wanted to create and feel with others.

Pivotal Moments: Finding Accidental Motivation with Steve Lawton
Before I left Brookdale, I had the distinct pleasure of a visit from Steve H. Lawton, a multifaceted individual with a background ranging from aerospace engineering at NASA to business executive roles at Dell. Thanks to a connection through Milo Hamilton, who worked with the ad agency promoting Steve's book *Head First*, we were able to arrange this fortuitous meeting. What made Steve's visit exceptionally impactful was how our experiences aligned; we were both survivors with powerful stories to share. We spoke at length about our respective accidents, finding common ground in a way that only those who have faced similar hardships can. What's even more remarkable was that during our conversation, the idea for my own memoir began to crystallize. In a moment of shared insight, the title "Accidental Motivation" came to me—serving as a reminder of my journey and how I used my accident to propel me forward. The visit wasn't just a nice gesture, it got me thinking and helped me heal.

From Dependency to Self-Sufficiency: The Role of a True Friend

As my time at Brookdale drew to a close, Hollie took an active role in my transition plans. My ultimate goal was to regain my independence, yet it was apparent that I couldn't handle the responsibilities of daily living on my own. My former wife had her own set of responsibilities, my siblings were too far away in Ohio, and among my friends in Austin, Hollie was a standout. She had been my rock for the last two months.

The day of my discharge arrived and I was greeted by a crowd of people who had been there with me, through thick and thin. Among them were my friends and cycling companions from that life-changing day. It was a profound reminder that life is a journey filled with ups and downs, best navigated with the support and love of those around us.

Hollie and her daughter welcomed me into their home. The preparation for this shift had been thorough. A member of Brookdale's staff had joined us to assess the accessibility and safety features of Hollie's residence. She'd gone the extra mile, installing a shower bench and motion-activated lights in essential areas. Little did I know, these simple additions would be invaluable, particularly when I found myself waking up every forty-five minutes to use the bathroom due to what later seemed to be a mistaken prescription for a diuretic.

Dr. Martin Molina had always been my doctor and became my go-to medical professional post-discharge. He marveled at my survival, reading the first few pages of my hospital discharge papers, remarking, "I can't believe you are alive." He recommended adhering to my medication schedule, getting plenty of sleep, and following a rigorous regimen to aid my recovery. He emphasized that maintaining a regular schedule was crucial. "I want you to go to bed at the same time each night and get up and out of bed early each morning." This advice sounded deceptively simple until I attempted to put it into practice.

My day began at 7:00 AM, aligning with Hollie and Montannah's school morning routine. Given my condition—weighing a mere 155 pounds and severely weakened—the mornings were a monumental task. Shuffling from the bedroom to the family room and then to the dining area was an exhausting circuit. Compelled more by necessity than interest, I would watch the morning news and struggle through a breakfast that hardly appealed to me, before retreating to the bedroom for some much-needed rest. Initially, managing to sit upright was a feat I could only sustain for about ten to fifteen minutes. Despite its monotony, this routine was non-negotiable, and I forced myself to adhere to it during those grueling first two months.

A week into my recovery at home, I started with in-bed physical therapy exercises aimed at mobilizing my arms and legs. By the second week, the regimen had escalated—I was climbing stairs to the second floor and venturing outside for brief walks.

During the third week, the therapy shifted settings to the kitchen, focusing on my dexterity in handling dishes and utensils. To me, these exercises felt rudimentary, as though tailored for someone permanently homebound. Yet again, we took to the outdoors for a marginally longer walk than before. Upon our return, my therapist announced that I had achieved 'ambulatory' status. Her words left me puzzled until she clarified: in her eyes, I could now walk independently, signaling the nearing end of her role in my recovery. Her upbeat assessment stoked not satisfaction, but a burning resolve within me. Merely shambling twenty yards didn't qualify as 'recovery' in my book. It motivated me to push myself even harder.

Frustrated by the incremental progress, I called for a comprehensive evaluation. The agency dispatched Tyler Fleck, a credentialed in-home physical therapist, to assess my condition. Tyler's advice was both straightforward and emphatic: "You need a specialized hand therapist for your right hand and outpatient therapy for your leg. In-home care simply won't suffice."

During his assessment, he instructed me to 'walk' my fingers up the wall to gauge the condition of my right shoulder. I was taken aback when pain forced me to halt midway. This uncomfortable moment unearthed a powerful memory—recalling my mother's struggle with physical therapy after her mastectomy. The similarities between her journey and mine became inescapably evident.

Tyler stressed the critical need for outpatient therapy to avert the possibility of my shoulder and leg becoming immobile and potentially never fully recovering. The fact that I couldn't lift my arm served as a startling alarm bell—my condition was regressing, not getting better.

Opting for outpatient physical therapy proved vastly more effective for several reasons: it offered specialized equipment, a regimented setting, a certified hand specialist, and intensive, frequent sessions that sped up my rehabilitation process.

However, there was the logistical challenge of getting to these appointments. Since I wasn't in a condition to drive, the responsibility fell on Hollie and a few other friends. The litany of healthcare professionals I needed to consult was extensive, including an orthopedic surgeon, a neurologist, a cardiologist, a hand therapist, a general physical therapist, a dentist, and my primary care physician.

The Healing Power of Small Victories

Few people experience a life-altering moment that catalyzes change. I feel fortunate to have had the opportunity to change after surviving both physical and mental injuries. My healing was slow, granting me hundreds upon hundreds of hours of introspective solitude. Most days brought small wins that slowly but surely improved how I felt both physically and mentally. Within a matter of weeks, my bones could bear weight again, and my ability to remember began to improve as the fog in my mind slowly lifted. Hollie provided a welcoming space to convalesce. She cooked my meals and attended to my needs.

Performing even basic tasks like showering became elaborate undertakings, as I was operating with one minimally functioning arm. Initially, Hollie had to assist me in every aspect of the process, from wrapping my right arm in plastic to helping me wash and dry.

The reality of needing assistance for such basic activities was both humbling and challenging.

To include me in her daily routine, Hollie modified her own schedule. While my natural inclination was to remain in bed, she was a source of constant encouragement. For my first venture outdoors, she set up a chair at the end of her driveway, inviting neighbors to get to know me. Though slightly awkward at first, it was invaluable therapy. I lasted just fifteen minutes that day before fatigue overtook me, and I used it as an excuse to go back inside and nap.

Motivated by Hollie's unwavering support, my increasing boredom, and a growing restlessness, I eventually started to explore the outdoors. Initially, my ventures were short—just to the end of the street and back. Gradually, these expanded to accompanying Hollie on walks to Montannah's school. As days turned into weeks, my confidence soared, allowing me to undertake solo strolls. Starting with just a single lap around our street, I progressed to two, then three laps, before finally gathering the courage to venture onto adjacent roads and even completing a full loop around the block. While I wasn't walking fast or anything, just being able to go farther thrilled me and I started walking more often.

Moments of Triumph and Tribulation

Due to the terms of my divorce agreement, my children were scheduled to stay with me every Thursday and every other weekend. However, the practicalities of my recovery meant that these plans had to be altered, leading to shorter, more constrained visits while I stayed at Hollie's place. To make the best of this situation, Hollie and I orchestrated an evening where I could spend quality time with my kids in the familiar surroundings of my own apartment.

On the night of November 21, 2016, Hollie dropped me off for a solo night at my own place and my former wife brought the children for what was to be a longer dinner engagement. It felt exhilarating to be in my own home again. Cooking had never been my strong suit, so my kids were not surprised when I proposed Kraft Macaroni and Cheese as our dinner option.

The ensuing incident served as a jarring wake-up call to the delicate condition of both my mind and body. Instead of adding macaroni to the boiling water, a mental lapse led me to pour in the dry cheese powder. The pot became a childhood volcano science project, spewing a fountain of orange "lava" all over the stove. My children caught my surprise and confusion as I hastily reached for a towel to contain the mess. They were too engrossed in their video games to make much of it, and I tried to pass it off as a minor mishap. However, the realization of what I had done filled me with a sense of foreboding, making me increasingly cautious about the potential for future mistakes.

Two days later, on November 23rd, Hollie, Montannah, and I went out for dinner to commemorate my fifty-third birthday. It was a bittersweet occasion, as it marked the first time I was celebrating without my former wife and children. We engaged in small talk while ordering our food. When my steak was served, it quickly became evident that my one functional hand wasn't up to the task of cutting it. Hollie, sensing the challenge, immediately leaned over and sliced the steak for me, emulating the nurturing care a mother provides for a child in need. While I was appreciative of her considerate gesture and the special birthday dinner, I wasn't sure if I managed to hide my underlying sadness.

Hollie is a person of extraordinary empathy and generosity, frequently dedicating herself to charitable endeavors and orchestrating volunteer opportunities. Fast forward to December 6, 2016, when she coordinated a volunteer team to assist with a holiday dinner for the Any Baby Can organization. Our group of fourteen manned a few tables, distributing food to those less fortunate. The evening was enlivened by charitable spirit, and my daughter Katherine joined us, adding her own youthful enthusiasm to the effort.

The occasion was meaningful, but it was also a glaring signpost on the long road of my recovery. It marked the second time I'd stepped away from the cocoon of Hollie's home since the accident. Midway through the event, fatigue overwhelmed me; standing any longer was not an option. I had to take a seat, and soon after, I retreated to the car to lie down and rest. The night offered me a brief glimpse of normality, promptly followed by a now all-too-familiar nap, reminding me that my journey toward full recovery was far from over.

During the recovery process from a life-altering accident, it's not uncommon for someone to find themselves disinterested in activities that once brought them joy. This could be attributed to a range of factors, including physical limitations, emotional trauma, fear, shifted priorities, or even cognitive changes. In my case, I found myself disinterested in three activities that used to be central to my life: alcohol, sex, and cycling. It was not until eight months had passed that I took my first sip of alcohol, and a striking 1,005 days later, I finally felt prepared to mount a bike for a celebratory outdoor ride with Tom Lawrence.

Sexuality was another aspect of life that was impacted. My doctor underlined its significance and spoke frankly about the possible repercussions of avoiding sexual activity. He advised me to engage in masturbation, a recommendation that Hollie, my caregiver, also endorsed. Despite my initial reluctance, Hollie guided me with gentle encouragement to confront and eventually overcome my mental barriers. When I finally achieved that milestone, the emotional weight of the moment brought me to tears. Although it was a challenging subject to tackle in my memoir, this episode became a pivotal point in my journey to recovery. It broke the illusion that some parts of me had been irrevocably lost due to the accident.

Rediscovering Independence and Connection on the Road to Recovery
Hollie was as generous as a friend could be to me, but I knew that my dependence on her was a burden and so in January 2017, I returned to my own apartment to continue the next chapter of my recovery. The Chevrolet Avalanche, the same one I had driven to that ill-fated Labor Day Bat City ride, had been idly sitting in

the parking lot since the accident. Hollie helped me change its dead battery. Once she left, I gathered the courage to slide into the driver's seat, start the engine, and cautiously make a lap around the apartment's parking area. The experience was tinged with fear, but the exhilaration of reclaiming some semblance of mobility after months of dependence was immeasurable.

The initial two weeks were spent reacquainting myself with my home, addressing my basic needs, and preparing my own meals. However, when darkness set in, so did episodes of depression. I found myself yearning for human connection, reaching out to friends, family, and even my former wife to escape the weight of my solitude. Looking back on that period of almost complete isolation, it's staggering to realize the emotional toll it took.

On the evening of January 9, 2017, my recovery journey took a sharp, disheartening turn. A severe infection in my right elbow reached a critical stage, requiring emergency surgery. The gravity of the situation gripped me with the fear that I could lose my right arm. During the procedure, Dr. Hill removed a significant amount of infected and necrotic tissue, in addition to removing previously implanted screws and the artificial titanium radial head. He stressed the increased risk of sustained infection due to the tendency of bacteria to attach to foreign materials. Waking up after the grueling five-hour operation, all I cared about was whether I still had my arm, and I was consumed by the worst pain I had ever felt.

Just two days later, I was back in the operating room due to the complicated nature of the infection and heterotopic ossification (HO) in my elbow, a condition involving abnormal bone growth in non-skeletal tissues. Dr. Hill removed more tissue, and Dr. Brent Egeland, a reconstructive hand surgery expert, performed a nerve transposition. This complicated process involved connecting a functioning nerve to my damaged ulnar nerve, with the aim of restoring nerve signals to the muscles of my hand. Despite these efforts, the exterior of my lower right arm largely remains numb, and I barely have any sensation in the ulnar portion of my right hand. The act of typing continues to be a cumbersome task.

In the battle against drug-resistant bacteria, Dr. Fida Khan, an infectious disease specialist, formulated a three-stage antibiotic regimen delivered via a peripherally inserted central catheter (PICC) line. Initially, I received a three-hour IV drip of Zosyn, followed by a dose of Tobramycin—a powerful drug carrying risks of kidney failure. The final stage involved a two-month course of self-administered Cefepime. Throughout this period, I followed a strict schedule and routine for cleaning and flushing the PICC line, administering the antibiotics through a specialized pump, the Halyard Homepump Eclipse, every eight hours.

The ordeal of rehospitalization felt like a cruel setback in my recovery. I pleaded for discharge on the eighth and ninth days following the surgeries, only to be released on January 17th. The cost of my newfound freedom was a burdensome responsibility: the need to self-administer antibiotics for the next two months.

On the 8th of March 2017, I was ecstatic and relieved as I concluded my two-month antibiotic regimen. Completing my final dosage, I prepared myself for the removal of the PICC line that had been a constant presence in my life. With slight apprehension, I sanitized my hands before gripping the blue end of the line that jutted out from my left arm. As I tugged it gently, the line started to glide out from the vein. A momentary pause overtook me, as I considered the proximity of the other end of this line to my heart, but there was no going back. Extracting the twenty-four-inch line, I was met with a modest spatter of blood. The sensation of liberation that followed was unparalleled as I was free from the procedure that had limited my movements mostly to my home for the last sixty days.

Nevertheless, the medical saga didn't end with the removal of the PICC line. I experienced two more, albeit less intense, infections later that year, which were treated with oral Doxycycline Monohydrate anti-biotics, adding another twist to my already complicated health history.

The healing process is rarely straightforward. Months later, I encountered another challenge: a recurrence of HO, where abnormal bone growth was again fusing two bones in my forearm, inhibiting my ability to rotate my hand. I needed another surgery, which Dr. Hill performed. This time, Dr. Egeland also repositioned the ulnar nerve to alleviate tension and potentially improve the function of my lower arm and hand.

Rediscovering Life Through Walking

On the morning of January 31 at 6:38 AM, I strapped on my Garmin watch to record my walking activity for the first time. My watch's log shows that I completed four loops around a section of my apartment complex's parking area, covering a total distance of 1.16 miles at a pace of 24:09 minutes per mile. This routine rapidly evolved into my primary means of breaking the monotony of recovery, providing much-needed physical exercise and mental relief.

Walking became a sanctuary for me. Triggered by my Garmin watch's hourly stand-up alert, I sometimes found myself looping the parking lot six to ten times a day, covering over three miles at times. This walking ritual was not just an escape; it provided the mental space I needed to deeply reflect on and absorb the truth about my life: I was unfulfilled and deeply unhappy. Had I been content, the near-brush with death would have been met with acceptance rather than fear. The experience revealed to me that I had spent years chasing material success at the expense of inner fulfillment and meaningful relationships.

From that point on, living my old life wasn't an option. Before the accident, I had lived by what I assumed were life's rules—navigating work challenges, marital struggles, and family demands. While I felt grateful for my life, there was an undercurrent of unspoken sadness, a profound lack of fulfillment.

The accident laid bare another humbling truth: the illusion of control over my bike, my choices, and even my life, was just that—an illusion. So many factors contributed to my survival that day, from first responders to simple timing, and none were of my doing. What, then, did I truly control?

Walking and Talking: A New Chapter with My Son

During my home recovery, I was able to connect with my children more than before. Perhaps my vulnerability and diminished independence made me more accessible to them. I let my guard down and openly expressed my love for each of them. One day, I asked my son to walk with me during his visit and to my surprise, he agreed. We completed a 1.3-mile loop around the entire parking lot, spending about half an hour immersed in conversation. That walk marked the longest stretch of one-on-one dialogue I could recall having with him, and I cherished every second of it. We discussed various subjects, including my recovery and the value of my walks, his experiences at school, and our family separation, among other things.

I shared with John August that he was about the same age as I was when my father passed away. While I'm not sure the gravity of that fully settled in for him, it didn't matter. What was important was the present moment, where he still had his dad actively participating in his life. It led me to a realization: too often, as parents, we try to navigate our children's lives based on our own past experiences, rather than recognizing the distinct challenges they face. By staying an active part of my son's life, I hoped to spare him the emotional hardships I had experienced. That was the best I could do.

Our walking ritual continued for several months until his interest waned. Though the walks ceased, our warm, affectionate hugs whenever we meet have endured.

One particularly amusing interaction happened in 2021 when I invited him to accompany me on a hiking trip into the Grand Canyon. After weeks of hemming and hawing, he finally blurted out in frustration, "Dad, I don't know why you like walking outside so much." It remains one of my favorite memories and serves as an ongoing personal challenge: I'm determined to one day hike the Grand Canyon with him by my side.

My recovery at home, alone, allowed me to focus on what was best for me, which fits with my life philosophy. My focus was laser-sharp: I wanted to live, to heal, and to walk again. It wasn't until I'd secured my own oxygen mask, so to speak, that I could turn my attention outward to other crucial life matters, such as my children and the meaningful relationships that enrich my existence.

My Return to Community: A Coffee Shop Reunion

On February 11, 2017, I remember what felt like my first meeting with Christie, although she had actually visited me in the hospital. After months of social isolation, mainly interacting with close friends and family, I decided to join the Bat City Cycling team at Red Horn Coffee that Saturday morning, ahead of their 8 AM ride.

However, the journey to the coffee shop presented its own set of challenges. Unwittingly, I ended up navigating the daunting two-lane stack interchange between highways TX-620 and TX-35. Suspended about 100 feet in the air, an abrupt wave of dread washed over me. I had to stop my truck right between the lanes. What I didn't know then was that I was undergoing a mild panic attack. My heart pounded in my chest, my gaze nervously scanning the dizzying heights and the void beyond the barriers. Luckily, no cars were behind me, giving me a moment to regain my composure. Gripping the wheel tightly, I cautiously pressed the gas pedal, guiding my truck down toward solid ground This brief but intense episode left its mark; for the next half year, I avoided crossing bridges.

My recollections of arriving at Red Horn are somewhat hazy, yet I distinctly remember grabbing a cup of coffee. Tom Lawrence, always an early bird, found me and offered a comforting hug. He stayed close as others—some who had been with me on that fateful ride—came over, expressing their awe at my recovery. Their enthusiasm was heartening but also draining. Within forty-five minutes, I was exhausted. Just before the group set off, I stepped out for a group photo, smiling widely. As the group rode away from the parking lot, I was overcome with a profound sense of gratitude simply because I was alive.

The accident forever changed me, both physically and mentally, and brought together three key components for change: the drive to improve, the time to do it, and a roadmap for how to get there. My heart was stronger than I ever realized, which enabled me to survive that fifty-foot fall. Even though my bones healed, they didn't do so perfectly. My hands have lasting nerve damage that reminds me of what I went through every time I type. The changes in my brain also changed how I see life, but I don't see myself as a victim; I am a proud survivor and my new way of looking at things pushes me to find answers to questions I used to ignore.

SELFISH HAPPINESS
(MY PHILOSOPHY)

"It's not selfish to love yourself, take care of yourself, and to make your happiness a priority. It's necessary."
— Mandy Hale

Awakening From Unhappiness

After my accident, I wrestled with questions like, 'Why am I here?' and 'Do I have control?' The answers to these questions were as elusive as those regarding why my father was taken from me when I was ten. I also felt a profound sense of unhappiness and dissatisfaction. I came to realize that change was essential. In my pursuit to evolve to a place where I would feel happier and perhaps better understand life, I began to formulate a concept that I coined Selfish Determinism, a unique perspective that, for me, sheds light on the fundamental forces that govern our universe and challenges traditional notions of free will and fate.

The concept of Universal Order posits that all elements in the universe adhere to fundamental physical laws. As intricate and complex beings, humans are merely highly organized and predictable creatures, guided by these same universal laws. Our thoughts and subsequent actions are not independent choices. Rather, they are responses to prior events and existing circumstances.

I began exploring the influences in my life and came to realize how much they controlled my decisions, my reactions. I also discovered the harsh reality that I never truly had any choice or free will. The philosophy of causal determinism took on new meaning for me.

The brain's ability to make predictions and respond doesn't mean we have free will. Decision-making is a methodical process where we utilize our knowledge, weigh options, and consider outcomes. In every situation, no matter how complex, people make what they believe to be the best decision given their circumstances. But there is really only one choice or one option available, and that choice, by default, becomes the best choice. From this perspective, every decision you have ever made in your life was, in fact, the best decision you could have made.

I view my past decisions, really all of my decisions, as the best decisions I could have made given the scope of my knowledge and circumstances. When I hear the phrase "If only I knew then what I know now," I can't help but regard it as a wasted sentiment. It may sound simplistic, but I believe that each person's decisions are the best they can make, as they are based on all the knowledge they have at the moment of decision-making. Because we make decisions based on what we know in the moment, there is no reason to regret past decisions. Our past should be a source of wisdom, as our accumulated knowledge influences and shapes our future.

In my youth, I didn't fully grasp my own capabilities or the reality around me. While I believed I was actively making my own choices, I now see that I was more of a passive spectator in my own life. Like driftwood floating down Wolf Creek, my life's journey has been shaped by the places I've been, the people I've encountered, and many cultural influences. Although I believed I was making choices, I now understand that these choices were dictated by the context of the situation.

As I peeled back the layers of my life in 2016 after my accident, I began to understand the cumulative effect of these lifelong influences and how the path of my whole life led to profound unhappiness. I sadly realized that falling off a bridge and almost dying unhappy was my destiny. I could not have stopped it. Instead of falling into despair, however, I decided that figuring out how to prioritize my own happiness was the only reason to live.

Selfish Determinism

The life philosophy I call **Selfish Determinism** blends two concepts: a self-interested individual navigating life in a causally determined universe.

Selfishness, according to Merriam-Webster, is described as an excessive focus on oneself, pursuing personal gain or pleasure without regard for others. I hold the belief that being selfish is essential for survival and happiness. Many things can be construed as selfish or in our self-interest:

If we do something for someone hoping for a favor in return, we are being selfish.

If we do something for someone because it makes us feel good, we are being selfish.

If we do something because of religious beliefs or divine command, we are being selfish.

If we care more for our own child than other children, we are being selfish.

If we aim to make our spouse happy because it brings us happiness, we are being selfish.

I urge you to keep an open mind while I use these terms to describe my ideas. I solely use "selfish" and "selfishness" in a neutral and positive manner.

Being self-interested and embracing our unique needs and desires doesn't mean we lack consideration for others or empathy. In fact, any informed individual always considers others, even if it is not in a deferential way. The absence of consideration can only stem from a lack of awareness regarding others. Once awareness is established, consideration naturally ensues. While consideration doesn't necessarily equate to concern for others, there will always be some level of consideration as long as awareness exists. In this context, "selfish" simply means recognizing that fulfilling our own needs can lead to a happier and more fulfilling life, making us better partners, parents, friends, and citizens.

The traits of selfishness and self-interest have played a pivotal role in the survival and progress of the human species. When I prioritize my well-being and that of my family, or when I strive to become a better person, I am displaying acts of selfishness. Society influences people in complex ways that can encourage both selfless and selfish behaviors. Social norms and structures often reward cooperative actions with social approval or status, nudging people toward communal behavior. On the other hand, elements like competition and individualism also have a significant place in society, particularly in capitalist economies, promoting self-interested actions.

The primary laws of nature revolve around self-preservation, underscoring the fundamental significance of self-interest. While self-preservation is a key aspect of natural behavior, we also see examples of cooperation in human society, such as individuals donating anonymously to charities or firefighters risking their lives to save others. These seemingly selfless acts can indirectly support the individual's social standing or even psychological well-being, making the picture more complex than just pure self-interest.

In the context of Selfish Determinism, everything in the universe can be considered as acting in a selfish manner driven by a fundamental force of self-preservation that contributes to the balance of the universe. All things strive to continue existing, thus everything that exists contributes to universal balance.

From the Big Bang onward, laws of physics describe how the universe underwent rapid changes, each moment building upon the one before it. Starting from a point of intense heat and pressure, the universe expanded and cooled, leading to the formation of fundamental elements and eventually stars, planets, and even life as we know it. Determinism, a concept that can be traced back to ancient philosophical traditions, posits that every event is influenced by prior events. This has led to debates about the implications of determinism for human agency and the meaning or significance of our interests and desires, challenging traditional notions of randomness or free will.

While my theory of Selfish Determinism posits that everything is predetermined by prior events and individuals act in self-interest, it's worth mentioning that some scientific theories like quantum mechanics suggest a degree of randomness in the universe. According to quantum theory, certain events at the subatomic level are fundamentally random and not determined. However, how this quantum randomness scales up to affect our daily lives and choices is still a subject of debate among scientists and philosophers.

When faced with life's complexities, I found the principle of **Occam's razor**, attributed to the medieval philosopher William of Ockham (c. 1287–1347), to be a useful tool. This principle suggests that among competing hypotheses, the one with the fewest assumptions should be selected. That we are living in a deterministic universe makes the most sense, and we are right to question whether we have choice or free will. My philosophy combines the philosophy of determinism with our natural and biological self-interest.

The Five Tenets of Selfish Determinism

These principles serve as the cornerstone of my pragmatic worldview, shaping how I perceive and navigate reality. They enable me to determine what truly matters, what brings happiness, and what benefits those around me. Armed with this perspective, I now approach life with a different mindset and try to live within five tenets:

Tenet 1: **Self-interest** is not only natural but also necessary, and it promotes universal balance.

Tenet 2: **Causal Determinism** dictates that all events are the result of prior occurrences and natural laws, making the notions of individual control, willpower, and free will illusory.

Tenet 3: **Knowledge** empowers you to better understand your situation and influence your circumstances.

Tenet 4: **The Pursuit of Happiness** is a moral endeavor and aligns with the innate human desire for a life filled with purpose and fulfillment.

Tenet 5: **Happiness** is the ultimate goal of life, and the guiding principle of our actions and decisions.

As I developed my Selfish Determinism philosophy, I contemplated the significance of universal balance and influence—how life's give and take, both on a personal level and across the cosmos since the Big Bang, are essential for our reality to exist.

My Distinct Universe: The Rationality of Personal Choices

Looking back at my life with this new perspective, I realized that while many people follow a similar path, my experiences made my journey truly unique. My life, from growing up in Ohio to attending college and getting married, shares common experiences with many others. However, a unique combination of events—including the loss of my father, my mother's battle with breast cancer, my divorce at age fifty-two, and surviving a fifty-foot fall—have uniquely shaped my life. Each person's life is a culmination of individual circumstances and events, making it highly improbable for anyone else to have experienced life the same way. This uniqueness starts from our genetic makeup at birth and is continuously shaped by each experience, compounding and enriching our individuality. With this realization, I understand that my subjective reality is entirely my own, creating a unique universe where my decisions and actions make complete rational sense within the context of my life. Though others might perceive my actions as irrational, my actions are, in fact, entirely rational. Recognizing this and utilizing this knowledge can affect my future because my knowledge guides my actions, reactions, and the influences I exert. I can create a different future.

The Laws of Nature Exert Control Over Everything

There are numerous fundamental physical laws that govern the behavior of the universe. Some of the more well-known theories include Isaac Newton's theories of classical mechanics, which describe motion and the universal law of gravitation. Albert Einstein's theory of general relativity provides a comprehensive understanding of gravity and spacetime. The four laws of thermodynamics explain the principles of energy and heat transfer. Heisenberg's uncertainty principle relates to the limits of precision in measuring certain pairs of physical properties. Lastly, the Big Bang Theory offers an explanation for the origin and evolution of the universe.

A ball dropped to the ground is a simple example; the ball always falls with the same acceleration. Isaac Newton observed falling objects and later, based on his observations, proposed the law of universal gravitation, which posits that every particle attracts every other particle with a force that is proportional to the product of their masses and inversely proportional to the square of the distance between their centers. After others tested and verified his hypothesis, it became known as Newton's Law of Universal Gravitation. This concept of gravity even extends to the extreme conditions of black holes, where the gravitational pull is so intense that not even light can escape.

The relatively recent understanding that the Earth is not the center of the universe has dramatically shifted man's perception of what creates and governs our reality. In the past, people tended to overestimate their importance and place in the universe due to ignorance and a limited perspective. However, with the knowledge we have today, we realize that the number of planets in the universe is exceedingly large and likely inhabited by countless alien species. Scientific circles often describe us as "a speck of dust on a speck of dust," highlighting the vastness and humbling nature of our existence and that nothing is random.

Life unfolds in a somewhat predictable manner. Many of the events of today will likely repeat tomorrow and the day after. Basic physiological processes, like my heartbeat and breathing, continue reliably, as do natural phenomena such as changing seasons or precipitation. Even in high-stakes scenarios like skydiving, there's a level of predictability; for instance, I know the consequences of jumping without a working parachute. This pattern and predictability in life are valuable because they enable me to plan, and I can predict my reactions. While past experiences don't guarantee future success, they provide a framework for navigating future events, even if those events are already determined.

When Did You Have Control?

Think about why you decided to read this book, how you came across it, and why I wrote it. What is intriguing is that you had no influence over whether I would write this sentence or even create this book.

This book has already left an impression on you, and it will blend with countless other influences. Your reaction could vary from devouring the book to putting it down forever. Even if you stop reading, what you have already read will persist and influence you for the rest of your life.

So, the question is: When did you start making your own decisions in life? When did you take control? Imagine a hypothetical life journey. Your parents brought you into this world, took care of you by providing a home, food, water, affection, and a sense of belonging. Then, often with government assistance and influence, you received education from ages five to eighteen. This education, bolstered with your good grades, enabled you to attend college and earn a degree. With this degree, you secured a job you enjoy, relevant to your field of study. Life unfolded one step at a time, each leading to the next. You might have thought you were in control when you left your parents' house after high school, but consider the factors that influenced this decision and why. You'll find that many influences affected what you thought was an independent choice.

Causal determinism requires an understanding that every decision we make is not independent but rather a reaction to external influences. Our lives are a series of causes (reasons something happens) and effects (the result of those happenings). We cannot change why things happen or how something influences us; we can only recognize that we are influenced. Any decision might be influenced by numerous factors. So, it could be argued that your decision to attend college was less a choice and more a reaction to factors like reaching adulthood, growing older, financial constraints, and encouragement to leave your parents' home.

My memoir, *Accidental Motivation*, and **the understanding that life is determined**, with no free will, are external **influences** you can leverage to seek out and find happiness.

The Illusion of Free Will and the Reality of Unique Will

Most people grapple with the idea of "free will," wondering if we truly have control over our actions and decisions. The traditional notion of free will suggests that we are in charge, guided by our desires and the ability to predict and influence future outcomes. However, this idea is challenged by the deterministic view, which argues that all events are predetermined. In this framework, I introduce the concept of "unique will," a byproduct of a lifetime of experiences and interactions that makes each of us distinct.

Your will is individualized, shaped by your unique life story, comprising experiences, knowledge, and desires that no one else shares. While your decisions might seem like expressions of free will, they're actually predetermined responses influenced by your past.

For example, our emotional reactions to natural events like a sunny day or a violent storm are not under our control, yet they contribute to the fabric of our unique will. Even instinctual reactions—like pulling away from a hot surface—are not choices we make but outcomes pre-etched by nature and nurture.

It's crucial to recognize the limitations of our perceived freedom. Often, we're not aware that many elements of our lives are beyond our control. Take hunger, a biological cue for nourishment. Though it feels like we choose what to eat, the decision actually results from various influences such as availability, taste preferences, past experiences, and others' recommendations. We're not exercising free will but acting according to our "unique will."

As I sit here editing this manuscript, I'm acutely aware that my life's journey has led me to this exact moment. Every experience, every lesson, and every interaction has contributed to my unique worldview, affecting my future choices. Since no one else shares my life history, the decisions I make are rational within the context of my unique, subjective reality.

Over the years, a multitude of factors, including upbringing, friendships, education, and adult relationships, have sculpted who we are. All these influences combine to shape our unique will, which we often mistake for free will. This process isn't about making choices; it's about deterministic outcomes shaped by a complex web of past events.

While the universe operates on deterministic principles, our individual lives are guided by a set of influences and experiences that make us who we are. It's our personalized navigation system within a predetermined cosmos.

FINDING HAPPINESS
(APPLYING MY PHILOSOPHY)

"The purpose of our lives is to be happy."
— Dalai Lama

The Complexity of Pursuing Happiness

In this final chapter, I want to address a subject that perplexes many: the pursuit of happiness. The common belief that we're in complete control of our lives and choices often makes happiness seem elusive. This illusion of control places the onus entirely on us, feeding into the misconception that happiness is just another milestone to achieve through sheer willpower. Yet, in a deterministic universe where our lives are shaped by prior events and external factors, this approach can prove not only futile, but damaging.

The belief in free will can make the quest for happiness a contradictory and often stressful endeavor. When we operate under the assumption that we have full control, we're more likely to blame ourselves for not being "happy enough," adding unnecessary guilt or frustration to our emotional experience. The expectations we set for our happiness can become unrealistically high, setting us up for disappointment when the predetermined nature of our universe steers events in unforeseen directions. This cycle of expectations

and disappointments often leads to a state of perpetual dissatisfaction, as we endlessly chase after what we think will make us
happy, without ever arriving there.

Surrendering to the idea that many aspects of our life are beyond
our control might initially seem unsettling, but can ultimately be
liberating. By relinquishing the need to control every variable, we
create room for self-awareness, allowing ourselves the space to
identify what genuinely brings us joy and fulfillment. It's crucial
to understand that what makes one person happy doesn't necessarily do the same for another. Our unique experiences shape our
individual senses of happiness, influenced by relationships, career
satisfaction, personal values, and overall well-being.

Contrary to what some might think, the deterministic nature of
our universe doesn't rob us of the potential for happiness. Rather, it
guides us toward a more authentic experience of contentment—one
that isn't dependent on the illusion of control, but rather grounded in
a deep understanding of our role in the greater scheme of things. By
acknowledging the boundaries of our influence over events, we can
shift our focus toward appreciating what we do have and where we
currently stand in life. This form of acceptance can lead to a version
of happiness that is both more achievable and meaningful.

Finding Gratitude in the Mundane

Why do we so often overlook the simple joys that life offers? One
reason might be routine; we become so accustomed to our daily
comforts that we barely notice them. Take, for example, that daily
cup of coffee. It's not just caffeine in a cup—it's warmth in your
hands on a cold morning, a moment of solitude before a hectic
day, and an experience that could whisk you back in time. And yet,
most mornings, we sip it absentmindedly while scrolling through
emails or watching the news, missing an opportunity for a small
but meaningful moment of pleasure and gratitude.

Another reason we might take things for granted is ignorance,
particularly when it comes to the work or effort behind these

conveniences. How often do we pause to think about the labor that went into harvesting the coffee beans, the engineering behind the plumbing that provides us with instant hot water, or the intricate network of people and machines that brings electricity into our homes?

Furthermore, psychological factors like negativity bias can also play a role. Negativity bias is the human tendency to give more attention and weight to negative experiences than positive ones. This focus on what's wrong rather than what's right can rob us of the joy found in everyday experiences. In a world where bad news often overshadows the good, it's easy to become consumed by life's bigger challenges, inadvertently minimizing the smaller, positive experiences that happen on a more frequent basis.

During my time of healing and introspection, I learned the transformative power of mindfulness and gratitude. I began to understand that being present isn't just about acknowledging the monumental moments in life, it's also about cherishing the ordinary ones. When we allow ourselves to pause, to break from the automation of daily living, we open up a space to be thankful for the ordinary joys that fill our days, however mundane they may seem. This shift in focus, from what we lack to what we have, can alter our emotional landscape, fostering a deeper sense of happiness and fulfillment.

I'm in awe of how my life has evolved since the cycling accident. If someone had told me back then that I'd be sharing my journey and unveiling a novel philosophy called Selfish Determinism, I'd have been skeptical. Yet, it was that very accident that ignited my pursuit of deeper self-understanding.

We are where we are. Life has this uncanny ability to transform our darkest hours into opportunities for growth and renewal.

Personal Transformation
Being single since my divorce in 2016 and hoping to find someone with whom I could experience real happiness, I sought to apply my new philosophy and see what the universe had in store. When I

met my partner, Tina, in 2019, I knew I wanted a serious relation-ship with her from the start. My reaction to meeting her was to focus my attention solely on her. Although she was surprised at first, she quickly recognized that I was serious. The timing was right. We both were open to falling in love and embraced the possibility of a future together. The years with her have been the happiest of my life and have helped me put my philosophy of Selfish Determinism to work.

Committing to her from the beginning was different for me. I had never felt so strongly about making a relationship work, and I was self-interested. I wanted to do whatever was required to be in a relationship with her, and my approach worked. Our relationship has endured. She says we are lucky, but I say it couldn't have turned out any other way. My experience with being openly interested and committed in my relationship with Tina motivated me to practice a commitment mindset in other endeavors and relationships.

I began to reprioritize my interactions with my children as well. Instead of just spending time with them, I made a conscious effort to engage in activities that they enjoyed, fostering stronger connections and becoming an advocate for their own wants and desires. At eighteen, we cannot know that pursuing one's interests and passions leads to greater success and fulfillment in life, but as a parent, I feel I must do my best to impart this message to my children. Thus, when my son displayed impressive scores in the PSAT and SAT exams, I initially suggested he pursue a career in computer science. However, his heart led him to music education, drawn by the success of **Vandegrift High School Band** during his high school years. I wholeheartedly supported his decision, just as I supported my daughter's pursuit of aerospace engineering at **Embry-Riddle Aeronautical University**, an out-of-state college.

Instead of just talking or texting with friends and family on special occasions, holidays, and birthdays, I sought out shared interests and engaging activities when possible. Among my favorite things in life is hiking the **Grand Canyon**. It is a truly life-chang-ing experience. The view from the South Rim is breathtaking but stepping off the rim and hiking down into and along the Grand Canyon, one of many pursuits I affectionately call "sight-doing" instead of merely "sight-seeing," is transformative.

During the summer of 2021, I proposed the ambitious adventure of hiking the Grand Canyon to three of my closest high school friends. Though we had crossed paths occasionally over the years, meeting at class reunions and catching up over dinner and drinks during our visits to different cities, I longed for a more significant and unforgettable experience. These friends meant the world to me, and I craved the opportunity to spend extended quality time with them. The preparation and planning for this remarkable journey lasted over a year until finally, in September 2022, we gathered at the South Kaibab Trailhead.

Our plan was to hike seven miles down the South Kaibab Trail, spend a night in the historic Phantom Ranch Lodge inside the national park, and then climb ten miles out on the Bright Angel Trail the following day. Given the scorching Arizona summer, Mark Polston humorously dubbed it "Holsinger's Death March," and the nickname stuck. Jokes aside, as my friends began to understand the significance of this journey to me, they wholeheartedly joined in. Jeff Schwartz even jokingly remarked to a friend, "Holsinger almost died and now wants to hike the Grand Canyon . . . that's why we're doing it."

After completing the hike, we shared a flight back to our fortieth Brookville High School reunion. It was a perfect week of pushing our limits and creating memories with the people I love. Late that Saturday night, at the reunion, Barry Denlinger said, "The best part of this trip was spending time together with you guys." It became a cherished memory that I wouldn't have imagined before my accident, but for which I am now eternally grateful. I prioritized my relationships with my friends and found some of the happiest days of my life in the process.

Call to Action

Understanding the tenets of Selfish Determinism isn't merely an intellectual exercise; it has concrete ramifications for our daily lives. Let's talk about some real-world applications.

To begin with, by **acknowledging the deterministic factors at play**—such as upbringing, environment, and even genetics—we can **cultivate compassion for ourselves and others**. This can be particularly empowering in situations where societal judgment can be harsh, such as in cases of addiction, career setbacks, or failed relationships. Recognizing these deterministic influences can mitigate feelings of guilt or shame, creating a more empathetic perspective for both the individual and those around them.

Furthermore, Selfish Determinism **aids in personal growth**. Once you understand that **self-interest is a natural, deterministic impulse,** you can **channel it constructively**. Instead of lamenting this 'selfishness,' use it as a motivational force to propel you toward your goals, whether they're in personal development, career progression, or interpersonal relationships. Harness your self-interest to build habits that contribute to long-term happiness and well-being.

And finally, this philosophy provides a **mental framework for crisis management**. When life takes an unexpected turn—like my experience with my bicycling accident—it's easy to spiral into despair, thinking everything is your fault. Selfish Determinism offers an alternative narrative. It allows us to separate what's in our control from what's not, empowering us to **take actionable steps to improve our situation without being paralyzed by guilt or regret.**

By integrating the principles of Selfish Determinism into your life, you're not just acknowledging the deterministic universe we live in; you're making it work for you. You're taking the reins of the aspects of life that you can control, even if it's just your attitudes and responses, to steer yourself toward happiness and satisfaction.

Through my own experiences and the philosophy of Selfish

Determinism, I've come to understand that the journey to happiness is both predetermined and deeply personal. If you're struggling to understand how to be happier, here are some concrete steps based on what I've learned:

1. Get to Know You

Take some time to think about what actually makes you happy. What do you want to accomplish in life? Remember, happiness is a personal thing, so you've got to find out what really matters to you. Even when I was laid up in the hospital, hurting and broken, I found a reason to smile because I was just thankful to be alive. Don't feel bad about focusing on yourself; it's just how we're all wired. The better you know yourself, the easier it'll be to find what makes you happy.

2. Accept and Adapt

The events in your life are predetermined. Instead of lamenting your circumstances, learn to adapt. My accident taught me that no matter how much we plan, terrible and wonderful things happen—life happens. Adaptability and acceptance can be assets when determining how much you can control life and find happiness within it.

3. Build Your Support Network

One of the most valuable lessons I've learned is the importance of relationships. Interdependence enriches our lives in ways that solitary pursuits of happiness simply cannot. Lean on your relationships, be open about your feelings and your needs. Don't underestimate the value of giving and receiving support.

4. Maintain a Learning Mindset

Even if you think you've got it all figured out, you don't. Keep an open mind and continue learning from every experience and every individual you meet. I told myself many times that I was in control and had life all sorted, but if I have learned anything, it is that learning is a lifelong process.

5. Honesty Above All
One of the cornerstones of a fulfilling life is honesty, both with yourself and others. Contrary to the often-complicated webs we weave when we lie, honesty simplifies life.

6. Plan Your Route to Happiness
It's not enough to simply endure or survive life's challenges. Aim higher. Make a conscious plan for achieving your own happiness. During my time in recovery, I realized that merely 'getting by' wasn't fulfilling. So, make a roadmap that's tailored to your own needs and aspirations.

7. Value and Leverage Your Uniqueness
Although we all engage in mimicry and mirroring to some extent, your individuality is your superpower. Learn from others but remain true to yourself. Value your uniqueness and make the most of your personal strengths.

8. Recognize Your Cosmic Significance
Your very existence has an impact, both on those around you and in the broader tapestry of life and the universe. Don't underestimate the ripples you create in the lives of others and, more expansively, in the predetermined unfolding of the universe itself.

Final Thoughts
The accident on September 5, 2016, was a pivot point in my life. It led me to the philosophy of Selfish Determinism, which has been both a challenging and comforting lens through which to view my experiences. Understanding that my past was set in stone and my future is largely determined brings me peace. This realization has been a form of healing for me, and I hope sharing it might offer

you some insight as well.

Even in a deterministic universe, our reactions to life's curveballs matter. They don't just shape our own lives but also leave an imprint on those around us. This book is my way of inviting you into a new understanding of life's challenges and opportunities.

As you strive for happiness, remember that the pursuit is active, not passive. Prioritizing personal growth and self-love can be your guiding light through a maze of complexities. While life-altering experiences can act as catalysts for change, you don't need to wait for them to happen to take action.

In essence, happiness isn't a given; it's a quest. And this quest, with all its trials and triumphs, is what makes life rich and rewarding. You have the tools you need; the rest is about embracing the journey.

EPILOGUE

My accident changed my life in ways that I could never have imagined. Before the accident, I was an unhappy, high-achieving professional with a broken family who believed that success and achievement were the primary paths to happiness. But after my accident, everything changed.

At first, I was confused, then angry and frustrated with my situation. I was forced to confront my own mortality, how close I came to dying unhappy, and the feeling that the accident had taken away any ability to live a happy life . . . and yet, I was glad just to be alive. Over time, I learned that true happiness is achievable when we reflect and commit to ourselves and those around us.

I now realize that my accident was a blessing in disguise. It forced me to confront my beliefs, commit to my relationships, and discover a new way of living that is centered on happiness and fulfillment. I started to make choices based on what would make me happy rather than what would impress others or fulfill societal expectations. I learned to live in the present moment, to appreciate the people in my life, to ask for help when I need it, and to find joy in helping others. Happiness is more than something to pursue—it is the only thing worth seeking in life

I am grateful for the lessons that I learned and for the opportunity to share my story. To anyone who is struggling with their own challenges, I want to offer some answers and a message of hope. Life is not always easy and the situation you are in is not always your fault. The universe is in control, but you have influence. If you can learn to identify the positive and negative influences in life, you can find happiness by moving toward positive people and situations, even in the darkest of times.

Don't feel regret for the situation you are in. Keep learning by reading and exposing yourself to new opportunities. Slowly, one positive influence at a time. Keep moving forward and remember that happiness is always within reach.

ACKNOWLEDGEMENTS

Writing this memoir has been an incredible journey of self-reflection and healing, and I am immensely grateful for the remarkable individuals who have played a vital role in my life during and after my accident. Their support, compassion, and presence have shaped my recovery and inspired me to share my story. I would like to express my heartfelt appreciation to Hollie Kenney, my children, Tom Lawrence, and Tina Amberboy, each of whom has made an indelible impact on my life.

To Hollie Kenney, my guardian angel: thank you will never be enough. When I had my bicycle accident, you were there, offering me unwavering support, both physically and emotionally. Your dedication and expertise in helping me navigate the challenging path to recovery were nothing short of remarkable. Your encouragement, patience, and belief in my strength fueled my determination to overcome obstacles. I am forever indebted to you for helping me reclaim my life.

To my beloved children, my source of strength and inspiration, I am eternally grateful for your tireless love and support during the darkest moments of my journey. Through every hardship and struggle I faced, you were my motivation to heal. Your presence and encouragement carried me through the most challenging times. I love you more than words can express.

My deepest appreciation to Tom Lawrence, who has been a constant source of support from that fateful day forward. Both of us endured the same accident and found strength in each other's company as we navigated our separate but parallel paths to recovery, becoming the best of friends. Our many conversations about life and rehabilitation helped me remain positive and, perhaps for the first time, made me realize how important it is to care for and need one another. Your kindness, compassion, and enduring friendship have been an invaluable gift, and I am forever grateful.

Amid my healing journey, I met Tina Amberboy, the love of my life. To my soulmate, my rock, thank you for your love and support. You entered my life right on time, offering me a chance to have something profound and a renewed sense of hope for my future. Your belief in my dreams and the joy you bring to my life are immeasurable. Together, we have created a love story that continues to inspire me every day.

To my editor, Nayla Zylberberg, who believed in the power of my story, thank you for your guidance, insight, and enthusiastic commitment to bringing my memoir to life. Your thoughtful feedback and constructive suggestions have helped shape this book into its final form.

Lastly, I extend my appreciation to all the readers who have journeyed with me through these pages. Your support and interest in my story are truly humbling. It is my hope that by sharing my experiences, I can inspire others to find strength and resilience in the face of adversity.

With heartfelt gratitude,

John Holsinger

ABOUT THE AUTHOR

John Holsinger began researching and writing this book over a decade ago because of his unanswered questions and a stubborn inability to attain happiness. He felt stuck in the cogs of the American Dream and is hoping to encourage readers to look inward and examine their lives in a way that selfishly focuses on their happiness and growth.

After his horrific bicycle accident in 2016, John has used his time on sabbatical from his software and technology executive sales positions to reflect on a pressing question: What is happiness?

Growing up in rural Ohio, John learned the value of independence and self-reliance at a young age. After his father's death, he became the man of the house at a young age. The odd jobs he worked gave him a broad set of skills, and Midwestern values and work ethic became the foundation of his belief system. However, small town rural life was unfulfilling. He left home for college at the University of Cincinnati, and soon after started his professional career at IBM.

As he pursued the American Dream, his increased spending and ascent up the corporate ladder left him yearning for more. Disillusioned by his technology sales job, he began isolating himself from family and friends while focusing on his athletic pursuits.

John has always been active and such rigorous physical activity has brought him much joy. He is a lifelong recreational athlete, participating in his first endurance event, the Solvang Century 112-mile bicycle ride, in 1991. In 2000, he began running marathons until a foot injury forced him to cross-train and exclusively focus on bicycling and swimming in 2007. He began participating in triathlons, often placing in his age group, and occasionally winning at the local level. In 2008, he competed in the Ironman Vineman 70.3 triathlon in Santa Rosa, CA. During this time, he also started delving deep into happiness and philosophy research, hoping to find meaning in his life.

On September 5, 2016, during a group bicycling ride, he experienced a life-changing event. He fell fifty feet off a bridge, colliding with solid rock at forty miles per hour. His memory loss and mind-body recovery process gave him a unique perspective as he unraveled the purpose of life. A long path of research and discovery culminated in his memoir, *Accidental Motivation.*

He had to embrace a level of vulnerability he never thought he'd feel. The experience exposed his weaknesses and demonstrated the need for the support of people around him. His needs perpetuated the idea for a personal security and support application, Biopower Security, and the subsequent embarkation of a bold marketing campaign.

Today he enjoys wonderful and fulfilling relationships with his partner Tina and his three children. His focus is living in every moment of every day and spending his time engaging with the people he loves in shared new life experiences.

John's desire is that this book helps other people understand what is and is not in their control, what they are responsible for, and how they can change their lives to be as happy as possible.

ENDNOTES

1. Hunsicker, Paul Alfred, and Leonard Kessler. *Mr. Peanut's Guide to Physical Fitness.* Standard Brands Educational Service, 1967.

2. Darwin, Charles. *The Descent of Man.* New York: American Home Library, 1902.

3. Sauce, Bruno, Magnus Liebherr, Nicholas Judd, and Torkel Klingberg. "The Impact of Digital Media on Children's Intelligence While Controlling for Genetic Differences in Cognition and Socioeconomic Background." Nature News. Nature Publishing Group, May 11, 2022. https://www.nature.com/articles/s41598-022-11341-2.

4. "Miller's Law." Miller's law. changingminds.org. Accessed December 1, 2022. http://changingminds.org/disciplines/communication/articles/millers_law.htm.

Printed in the USA
CPSIA information can be obtained
at www.ICGtesting.com
LVHW041140290124
769705LV00003B/414

9 798989 532209